NAMIBIA
Travel Guide

20 23

With Flexible Itineraries Perfect for Every Kind of Travelers

Olivia S. George

NAMIBIA

TRAVEL GUIDE 2023:

A Journey Through Namibia's Natural Treasures, Wildlife, Landscapes, Culture, Traditions and Adventure

Olivia S. George

Table of Contents

Fun Facts:

Namibia is home to the world's oldest desert, the Namib Desert, which contains some of the tallest sand dunes on Earth, including the famed Dune 45, great for daring dune surfing and spectacular dawn vistas.

INTRODUCTION

Last summer, I embarked on an extraordinary vacation to Namibia, a region of magnificent landscapes and rich cultural history. With a feeling of enthusiasm and amazement, I chose to explore this lovely country with the support of a skilled guided tour. Little did I realize that this choice would lead me to find a world of exceptional beauty and experiences that left an unforgettable impression on my heart.

My voyage started in the bustling capital city of Windhoek, where I met my pleasant tour guide, who introduced me to the varied cultures and customs of Namibia. As we traveled into the country, I marveled at the sharp contrast between the contemporary urban and the untamed grandeur of Namibia's immense desert.

The first stop on our voyage was Sossusvlei, a strange sight of towering red sand dunes that appeared to touch the sky. Witnessing the dawn over the dunes was a mystical experience, as the warm colors of the sun bathed the desert in a beautiful light. Guided by our professional tour guide, we climbed up one of the dunes, feeling the soft sand under our feet until we reached the peak and peered at the magnificent vista below.

From Sossusvlei, we continued our expedition to Etosha National Park, a wildlife refuge that left me in awe of Mother Nature's grandeur. The guided safari drives enabled us to observe an astounding assortment of animals, including towering elephants, charming giraffes, and the elusive big cats. Each meeting was a chance to appreciate, as our experienced guide gave intriguing insights about the animals' behavior and the park's conservation initiatives.

The drive took us to Swakopmund, a lovely seaside town located between the Namib Desert and the Atlantic Ocean. Here, I was charmed by the town's unusual combination of German colonial architecture and lively indigenous culture. Our guided excursion featured exhilarating activities such as quad riding on the dunes and a catamaran trip where we spotted lively dolphins and seals in their natural environment.

As the sun fell on our extraordinary adventure, we entered Damaraland, where historic rock formations and traditional Himba communities greeted us. The guided trip gave us an intimate insight of the Himba people's way of life, their rituals, and their strong connection to nature. The humbling experience of engaging with these warm-hearted folks showed me the significance of conserving age-old customs in a fast changing society.

One of the highlights of the journey was our visit to a conservation facility devoted to safeguarding the endangered rhinos. Witnessing these majestic animals up close was a painful reminder of the significance of conservation efforts to conserve these species for future generations.

Throughout the trip, our guide's love for Namibia's natural and cultural legacy was infectious, making every moment an enjoyable and instructive experience. Their skill and passion brought depth and significance to every location we visited, turning a normal sightseeing vacation into an excursion of the heart and spirit.

As I think of my amazing time in Namibia, I am glad for the chance to have experienced this gorgeous country with a guided tour. The voyage not only opened my eyes to the world's beauty but also generated a profound respect for the fragile balance between nature and humans. Namibia's soul-stirring scenery, warm-hearted people, and spectacular wildlife have left an indelible mark on my heart, and I anxiously anticipate the day when I may return to this enthralling region and continue my exploration of its untamed beauties.

History of Namibia

Namibia's history is rich and varied, defined by significant changes that have formed the country into what it is now. From ancient civilizations through colonialism, war for independence, and post-independence growth, each period has played a key influence in the country's history.

Pre-Colonial Era

The Pre-Colonial Era in Namibia refers to the time before European explorers and conquerors arrived in the area. This era spans thousands of years and is defined by the existence of prehistoric hunter-gatherer groups and early pastoralists.

Hunter-Gatherer Communities: Namibia's Pre-Colonial history starts with the existence of indigenous San people, also known as Bushmen, who are thought to be the original occupants of the area. The San lived a nomadic existence, dependent on hunting and gathering for their livelihood. They had a deep awareness of the terrain and its resources, utilizing natural shelters and making rock art as a way of communication and expression.

Arrival of Pastoralists: Around the 14th century, Bantu-speaking tribes started to move into the region from the north. These tribes included the Owambo, Herero, Himba, Damara, and others. The Bantu-speaking people were agriculturalists and pastoralists, bringing cultivated crops and cattle to the area. Their villages were frequently more permanent compared to the nomadic San communities.

Contact and Cultural Exchange: As Bantu-speaking tribes advanced southward, they found the San people, leading to cultural exchange and contact between the two groups. Some San villages absorbed agricultural traditions from the Bantu-speaking tribes, while others retained their original hunter-gatherer lifestyle.

Organization and Trade: Over time, Bantu-speaking tribes built sophisticated social systems and structured civilizations. They formed a system of government, with tribal chiefs and leaders governing their villages. Trade networks formed, facilitating the interchange of products and resources between diverse communities. Coastal populations, such as the Nama, participated in commerce with Arab and European traders.

Rock Art & Cultural Significance: One of the most important legacies of the Pre-Colonial Era in Namibia is the extensive collection of rock art left behind by the San people. These rock paintings and carvings represent scenes of everyday living, hunting, and spiritual beliefs.

The art gives vital insights into the old cultural practices and beliefs of the region's first inhabitants.

Overall, Namibia's Pre-Colonial Era was defined by the cohabitation of many cultural groups, each contributing to the region's rich legacy. The hunter-gatherer traditions of the San and the agricultural techniques of the Bantu-speaking tribes established the basis for the country's cultural variety and continue to be an integral element of Namibia's identity today.

European Exploration and Colonization

European exploration and colonization of Namibia started in the late 19th century, when European countries attempted to extend their empires and exploit fresh resources and trade routes. This phase of history had a deep and enduring influence on the area and its indigenous inhabitants.

Portuguese Exploration: The coastal area of Namibia was originally explored by Portuguese navigators in the 15th century. Portuguese explorer Bartolomeu Dias was the first European to cross the Cape of Good Hope in 1488, opening up marine trade routes to the Indian Ocean. However, the Portuguese did not establish a permanent presence in the region.

German Colonial Rule: In the late 19th century, European interest in Africa surged during the Scramble for Africa. At the Berlin Conference of 1884-1885, European countries split Africa into spheres of influence, and Germany was handed jurisdiction over the region known as German South West Africa, present-day Namibia.

In 1884, German businessman Adolf Lüderitz bought property along the Namibian coast from a local Nama chief, laying the groundwork for German colonization. The German colonial authority aimed to utilize the region's natural riches, mainly diamonds and copper, and construct towns for German immigrants.

Harsh Colonial practices: German colonial control was marked by severe practices, including forced labor, land expropriation, and violent repression of local opposition. The Herero and Nama groups, in particular, suffered under severe treatment and were subjected to forced labor on farms and in mines.

The German military's reaction to the Herero and Nama uprisings in 1904-1908 led to one of the worst episodes in Namibia's history, known as the Herero and Nama Genocide. Thousands of indigenous people were slain, and many more were pushed into the desert where they suffered famine and dehydration.

South African Administration: After Germany's defeat in World War I, South Africa was awarded a League of countries mandate to manage Namibia in 1920. The South African government perpetuated many of the repressive practices of the Germans, resulting in greater expropriation of land and oppression of the indigenous people.

Resistance and Nationalism: Throughout the colonial era, the indigenous people opposed European colonialism and battled for their rights and territory. Various groups and leaders, such as Chief Hendrik Witbooi and Chief Hosea Kutako, pushed for the rights and recognition of the indigenous peoples.

Road to Independence: In the 20th century, nationalist groups formed, demanding independence from South African control. The South West Africa People's Organization (SWAPO), headed by people like Sam Nujoma, Andimba Toivo ya Toivo, and Hifikepunye Pohamba, became a significant movement campaigning for freedom.

The armed conflict and international pressure on South Africa finally led to the evacuation of South African forces in 1989, opening the path for Namibia's independence.

The age of European discovery and colonialism greatly affected Namibia's history, leaving a legacy of social, economic, and political issues. The harsh policies and violent conflicts throughout the colonial era had a lasting influence on the country, and the battle for independence and self-determination marked a turning point in Namibia's history toward nationhood and sovereignty.

South African Administration

The South African administration of Namibia started in 1920, after the end of German colonial authority. Under a League of countries mandate, South Africa was awarded power to manage Namibia, then known as South West Africa. This era lasted until Namibia's independence in 1990 and had enormous effects for the country and its people.

Policies and Control: South Africa's administration of Namibia was defined by policies that paralleled its apartheid regime at home. The South African government enacted racial segregation, discriminatory legislation, and the systematic mistreatment of the indigenous people. The purpose was to retain strong control over the land and its resources.

Forced Labor and Land Dispossession: The South African government perpetuated the exploitative tactics of the former German colonial state. Indigenous Namibians, mainly the Herero and Nama populations, were subjected to forced labor on farms and in mines, contributing to the increased loss of land and resources.

Bantustans and Reserves: In an attempt to maintain racial segregation, the South African government developed laws that formed distinct homelands, sometimes known as Bantustans, for various ethnic groups. These Bantustans were designed to be self-governing entities, but they were actually puppet governments serving the interests of South Africa.

Nationalist groups and Resistance: During the South African government, nationalist groups demanding for independence and self-determination gained strength. The South West Africa People's Organization (SWAPO) emerged as the dominant nationalist organization, demanding an end to South African sovereignty and the formation of an independent Namibia.

SWAPO's armed branch, the People's Liberation Army of Namibia (PLAN), participated in a lengthy armed battle against the South African military and its supporters inside Namibia.

International Pressure and Independence: International pressure against South African apartheid policies and the Namibian independence fight led to growing isolation and criticism of South Africa's conduct in Namibia. The United Nations played a vital role in recognizing SWAPO as the legal representation of the Namibian people.

Negotiations between South Africa, SWAPO, and other parties led to the signing of the New York Accords in 1988, which provided the basis for Namibia's independence. In 1990, Namibia attained independence, with Sam Nujoma becoming the country's first president.

Legacy: The South African administration of Namibia left an enduring legacy of social, economic, and political issues for the newly independent country. The practices of forced labor, land confiscation, and racial segregation had enormous consequences on Namibia's people, resulting in persisting socioeconomic imbalances that the government continues to confront.

Despite the hurdles, Namibia's independence gave optimism and opportunity for developing a democratic and inclusive country. The country started the process of healing, reconciliation, and nation-building, hoping to overcome the injustices of the past and establish a unified and prosperous future for all Namibians.

Struggle for Independence

The battle for independence in Namibia was a hard-fought and lengthy undertaking that lasted many decades. The South West Africa People's Organization (SWAPO), headed by leaders like Sam Nujoma, Andimba Toivo ya Toivo, and Hifikepunye Pohamba, emerged as the major nationalist organization calling for freedom.

Under South African governance, Namibia endured repressive laws, racial segregation, forced labor, and land confiscation. SWAPO's armed branch, the People's Liberation Army of Namibia (PLAN), participated in guerrilla warfare against the South African military and its supporters inside Namibia.

The international community played a key role in assisting Namibia's quest for independence. The United Nations recognized SWAPO as the legal representation of the Namibian people, leading to greater isolation and criticism of South Africa's activities in Namibia.

Negotiations between South Africa, SWAPO, and other parties led to the signing of the New York Accords in 1988, creating the groundwork for Namibia's independence. In 1990, Namibia attained independence, with Sam Nujoma becoming the country's first president.

The war for independence was a turning point in Namibia's history, leading to the foundation of a democratic and autonomous country. It displayed the endurance, resolve, and togetherness of the Namibian people in their quest of self-determination and liberation from colonial tyranny. Today, Namibia continues to build on the basis created by the battle for independence, aiming towards social improvement, economic prosperity, and national unity.

Independence and Post-Colonial Development

After winning independence on March 21, 1990, Namibia proceeded on a road of country-building and post-colonial development. The country faced several obstacles, including social injustice, economic imbalances, and the desire for reconciliation between different ethnic groups.

Democratic Governance: Namibia enacted a democratic constitution that created a multi-party system and guaranteed the preservation of human rights and basic freedoms. Sam Nujoma, a significant leader in the independence fight, became the country's first president, guiding the country through its early years of independence.

National Reconciliation: Namibia acknowledged the need for healing and reconciliation after decades of colonial oppression and military conflict. The government formed the Truth and Reconciliation Commission (TRC) to examine human rights crimes that occurred during the colonial and apartheid period. The TRC attempted to bring criminals to justice and give closure for victims and their families.

Social Development: Post-independence, Namibia made considerable gains in increasing access to education, healthcare, and social services. The government invested in infrastructure development, extending schools, hospitals, and basic amenities to rural and underdeveloped communities.

Land Redistribution: One of the main difficulties confronting independent Namibia was land reform. The bulk of arable land remained in the hands of a few, primarily white, commercial farmers. The government initiated land redistribution and resettlement schemes to resolve land ownership imbalances and boost agricultural growth for formerly disadvantaged populations.

Economic Growth and Diversification: Namibia's economy is mainly dependent on mining, notably diamonds and uranium, as well as agriculture and fisheries. To achieve sustained economic development, the government concentrated on diversifying the economy by developing tourism, manufacturing, and services industries.

Regional and International Engagement: Namibia actively engaged in regional organizations such as the Southern African Development Community (SADC) and the African Union (AU). The country campaigned for regional integration, peace, and stability in southern Africa. Namibia has participated in peacekeeping operations and had a role in settling regional crises.

Conservation and Environmental Protection: Namibia is recognised for its dedication to conservation and environmental protection. The country used novel conservation strategies, including community-based natural resource management and wildlife conservancies, to encourage sustainable development while maintaining its rich biodiversity.

Issues and Ongoing Efforts: Despite development, Namibia confronts ongoing issues, including economic disparity, unemployment, and the effect of HIV/AIDS. The administration continues to address these concerns via focused social initiatives and economic reforms.

Namibia's Transition to Democracy

Namibia's transition to democracy was a spectacular journey that culminated in the country's independence in 1990. The country's battle for self-determination and independence from colonial and apartheid oppression had a crucial role in defining this transformation.

Rise of Nationalist Movements: The South West Africa People's Organization (SWAPO) developed as the primary nationalist organization campaigning for Namibia's independence. SWAPO, under the leadership of personalities like Sam Nujoma and Andimba Toivo ya Toivo, garnered support both locally and abroad.

Military Struggle and International Pressure: SWAPO's military branch, the People's Liberation Army of Namibia (PLAN), engaged in guerrilla warfare against the South African regime and its supporters inside Namibia. The battle for independence garnered worldwide attention and support, leading to further isolation and criticism of South Africa's conduct in Namibia.

Negotiations and the New York Accords: International pressure, along with the desire for a peaceful conclusion, led to discussions between South Africa, SWAPO, and other players.

The New York Accords were signed in 1988, providing the groundwork for Namibia's independence. A United Nations Transition Assistance Group (UNTAG) was dispatched to supervise the implementation of the Accords.

Democratic Constitution and Institutions: Namibia approved a democratic constitution that entrenched basic human rights, including the ability to vote and freedom of speech. The multi-party system was developed, encouraging political plurality and a dedication to peaceful and democratic administration.

Reconciliation and Nation-Building: Namibia acknowledged the need for reconciliation and healing after decades of colonial oppression and military conflict. The government formed the Truth and Reconciliation Commission (TRC) to examine human rights atrocities perpetrated during the colonial and apartheid period, intending to bring offenders to justice and give closure for victims.

Namibia's transition to democracy was a turning point in the country's history, moving from a past of oppression and struggle to a future of freedom, democracy, and national unity. The peaceful settlement and dedication to democratic ideals have created the framework for a stable and inclusive society, where Namibians continue to strive towards a brighter future for all residents.

Contemporary Namibia

Contemporary Namibia refers to the present-day situation of the country after attaining independence in 1990. It is a place of various cultures, breathtaking landscapes, and constant attempts towards growth and advancement.

Political Stability and Democracy: Namibia has maintained a stable political climate since achieving independence. The country runs under a democratic system with multi-party elections and a constitution that promotes human rights and basic freedoms.

Economic expansion and Diversification: Namibia's economy has undergone consistent expansion throughout the years, driven by industries like mining (diamonds, uranium), agriculture, fishing, and tourism. Efforts to diversify the economy and foster private sector growth are underway to lessen dependence on established industries.

Social Development and Education: Namibia has made progress in enhancing access to education, healthcare, and social services.

The government invests in educational facilities and efforts to promote the quality of education and give equitable opportunity to all residents.

Land Reform and Redistribution: Land reform is a major subject in Namibia. The government continues to execute land redistribution and resettlement projects to redress historical land ownership imbalances and empower formerly disadvantaged populations.

Conservation & Environmental Protection: Namibia is noted for its dedication to conservation and sustainable environmental practices. Community-based natural resource management and wildlife conservancies assist foster the coexistence of wildlife and human populations while maintaining biodiversity.

Efforts to Combat Poverty and disparity: Despite improvements, Namibia confronts difficulties of economic disparity and poverty. The government focuses on developing social initiatives and economic policies aimed at decreasing poverty and supporting equitable development.

Regional and International Engagement: Namibia actively engages in regional and international organizations, contributing to peacekeeping operations and lobbying for regional integration, economic cooperation, and sustainable development in southern Africa.

Infrastructure Development: Namibia has invested in improving its infrastructure, including road networks, communication systems, and renewable energy initiatives. These upgrades enhance connection and economic growth across the country.

Health and HIV/AIDS: Namibia has made substantial efforts in tackling public health concerns, particularly the effect of HIV/AIDS. The government has developed several programmes to offer treatment, assistance, and awareness campaigns to curb the spread of the illness.

Contemporary Namibia is a country that accepts its unique past while working to achieve a successful and cohesive future. Despite hurdles, Namibia continues to achieve progress in different sectors, led by the aim of a democratic, inclusive, and sustainable society for all its residents.

GETTING TO KNOW NAMIBIA

Geography and Climate

Namibia's geology and climate are as varied as they are compelling, presenting a spectacular assortment of landscapes and weather patterns across the country.

Geography: Namibia is situated in southwestern Africa and is surrounded by Angola to the north, Zambia and Zimbabwe to the northeast, Botswana to the east, and South Africa to the south and southeast. To the west, Namibia features a lengthy coastline along the Atlantic Ocean, known as the Skeleton Coast.

The country's landscape is characterized by enormous deserts, wide plains, rocky mountains, and arid riverbeds. The Namib Desert, one of the oldest deserts in the world, spans along the western coast, including towering sand dunes and distinctive desert-adapted vegetation and animals.

Moving north, the scenery shifts to the central plateau, which hosts the capital city, Windhoek. The plateau is interspersed with steep mountains and lush valleys. The eastern half of Namibia comprises the Kalahari Desert, a semi-arid area with grassy plains and scattered acacia trees.

In the northeastern part of Namibia is the Caprivi Strip, a small strip of territory that runs between Angola, Zambia, and Botswana. This area is known for its lush flora and many rivers, notably the Zambezi and Chobe.

Climate: Namibia enjoys a generally dry to semi-arid climate, with varied temperatures and rainfall patterns throughout the country. The climate may be categorized into three primary regions:

Desert Climate: The coastal area, including the Namib Desert, has a chilly desert climate, influenced by the cold Benguela Current. Summers are pleasant, and temperatures seldom reach 30°C (86°F). Fog and low clouds are abundant along the shore, supplying moisture to the desert-adapted vegetation and animals.

Semi-Arid Climate: The central plateau and most of the interior sections endure a semi-arid climate. Summers are hot, with temperatures reaching above 35°C (95°F), but winters are colder, with temperatures plummeting near freezing at night.

Subtropical Climate: The northeastern Caprivi Strip and certain places in the north enjoy a subtropical climate, with warmer temperatures and more rainfall compared to the rest of the country. Summers may be hot and humid, with temperatures regularly topping 35°C (95°F).

Namibia's climate is characterized by various seasons. Rainy season normally runs from November through April, with the highest rainfall in January and February. The remainder of the year is often dry and bright, making Namibia a perfect location for outdoor sports and wildlife watching.

Namibia's geology and climate contribute to its incredible beauty and unusual biodiversity, allowing tourists an opportunity to see a varied variety of landscapes and ecosystems that make this country a truly outstanding destination.

Wildlife and Conservation

Namibia is recognised for its abundant wildlife and devotion to conservation, making it a desirable destination for eco-tourism and wildlife aficionados. The country's wide and varied landscapes house a remarkable assortment of plant and animal species, some of which are specially suited to live in the harsh desert settings.

Iconic Wildlife: Namibia is home to a diverse variety of wildlife, including the "Big Five" game species: elephants, lions, leopards, rhinos, and buffalos. Other iconic creatures found in Namibia include cheetahs, giraffes, zebras, wildebeests, and numerous antelope species including springboks, oryx, and kudus.

Desert-Adapted Species: The Namib Desert is home to desert-adapted species that have evolved to live under dry environments. These include desert-adapted elephants, oryx, springboks, and the elusive desert-adapted lions. These remarkable creatures have evolved behavioral and physiological adaptations to deal with the harsh desert environment.

Etosha National Park: Etosha is Namibia's top wildlife park and one of Africa's biggest game reserves. It is distinguished by a huge salt pan, attracting a great assortment of species throughout the dry season. Visitors may watch animals congregating around waterholes, giving good possibilities for wildlife observation and photography.

Community-Based Conservation: Namibia is a pioneer in community-based conservation, where local people take a key part in maintaining and profiting from animal resources. Conservancies, community areas set aside for conservation and sustainable wildlife management, have been developed around the country. These projects assist in safeguarding animal habitats, support anti-poaching operations, and promote eco-tourism as a source of revenue for local people.

Efforts to Combat Poaching: Namibia has been successful in preventing poaching via strong anti-poaching measures and community engagement. The government and conservation groups work together to safeguard endangered animals, including rhinos and elephants, from unlawful poaching.

Conservation of Marine Life: Namibia's coastline is rich in marine life, sustaining a vibrant ecology of marine animals, including Cape fur seals, dolphins, and whales. Namibia has developed marine protected zones to maintain its varied marine wildlife and guarantee sustainable fishing methods.

Dark Sky Reserves: Namibia is noted for its clean night sky and little light pollution. Several sites, such as the NamibRand Nature Reserve and the Gamsberg Dark Sky Reserve, have been classified as dark sky reserves, giving exceptional chances for stargazing and astrophotography.

Namibia's dedication to wildlife conservation and sustainable methods has given it a position as a pioneer in eco-tourism and responsible wildlife management. Through community engagement, creative conservation projects, and strong anti-poaching measures, Namibia continues to safeguard its irreplaceable biodiversity for future generations to enjoy.

Conservation Efforts

Namibia has exhibited a great dedication to conservation activities, making it a worldwide leader in wildlife and environmental preservation. The country's conservation programmes are inspired by a goal of sustainable development and the safeguarding of its rich biodiversity.

Community-Based Conservation: Namibia's community-based conservation method engages local people in maintaining and profiting from animal resources. This strategy encourages communities to take ownership of conservation initiatives, contributing to the preservation of animal habitats and preventing poaching. Conservancies, created in common areas, have become crucial cornerstones of conservation and wildlife management.

Namibian Association of CBNRM Support Organizations (NACSO): NACSO plays a critical role in organizing and supporting community-based natural resource management (CBNRM) efforts. It works closely with local conservancies, offering technical knowledge, capacity-building, and promoting collaborations between communities and diverse stakeholders.

Rhino Conservation: Namibia has been successful in rhino conservation, notably with its black and white rhino herds. The government and conservation groups work together to fight poaching via powerful anti-poaching operations, tough law enforcement, and the use of technology to monitor and preserve rhinos.

Elephant Conservation: Namibia's desert-adapted elephants are a rare and cherished group. Conservationists and local communities unite to safeguard these elephants and their habitats, balancing the requirements of the creatures with the lives of people living in the area.

Animals Management Areas (WMAs): Namibia has developed Wildlife Management Areas (WMAs) to protect animals and their habitats on community property. These regions support sustainable land use practices, wildlife preservation, and eco-tourism, creating money for local populations and boosting conservation initiatives.

Marine Conservation: Namibia's marine conservation efforts concentrate on maintaining its unique maritime habitats and marine animal species, including seals, dolphins, and whales. The government has created marine protected zones to maintain its coastal biodiversity and encourage sustainable fishing methods.

Desert Lion Conservation: Namibia's desert-adapted lions are a fascinating subspecies that have evolved to living in the dry desert settings. Conservation groups watch and research these lions, working with local people to prevent human-wildlife conflicts and encourage cooperation.

Sustainable tourism: Namibia's tourist business stresses eco-tourism and ethical travel practices. Sustainable tourism programmes advocate minimum effect on the environment and cultural heritage while delivering advantages to local people via money generating and job possibilities.

Namibia's conservation initiatives have earned worldwide acclaim and appreciation, proving that the effective partnership between government, local people, and conservation groups can establish successful models of sustainable development and wildlife preservation. As a consequence, Namibia has become a shining example of how conservation and responsible environmental practices can coexist with socio-economic prosperity and enhance the lives of both people and animals.

PLANNING YOUR TRIP

Which Time of the Year is Best for Visiting?

The best time to visit Namibia mostly relies on your interests and the experiences you desire throughout your trip. Namibia's temperature and terrain fluctuate dramatically, giving various experiences throughout the year. Here are some concerns for various seasons:

Dry Season (May through October):
- This is the most popular period for travelers owing to the warm weather and fantastic animal watching chances.
- The temperatures are pleasant throughout the day, making it excellent for visiting the desert, national parks, and animal reserves.
- Game watching is best in areas like Etosha, since animals concentrate near water holes because of restricted water supplies.
- The skies are clear, allowing wonderful astronomy opportunities, particularly in authorized dark sky areas.

Cooler Months (June through August):
- Namibia's winter months enjoy colder temperatures, particularly during the nights and early mornings.

- This season is good for outdoor activities like trekking, since the weather is not too hot.
- Keep in mind that early morning game drives and activities may necessitate warm clothes.

Hot Season (November through April):

- This time of year is marked by greater temperatures, especially in December and January, which is the height of the summer season.
- While the days might be sweltering, this season gives a unique opportunity to experience the beautiful sceneries as the desert bursts with wildflowers following the rains.
- Birdwatching is wonderful during this season, as migrating birds arrive in the marshes and other habitats.

Rainy Season (January through April):
- Namibia's rainy season provides periodic showers and occasional thunderstorms, primarily in the northern and central areas.
- The desert regions may have low rainfall yet might be prone to flash floods in certain spots.
- Wildlife disperses during the wet season, making animal encounters less predictable in particular regions.

- However, this time of year gives a pleasant contrast to the scenery and might be intriguing to photographers and wildlife lovers.

Ultimately, the best time to visit Namibia depends on your choices for weather, wildlife watching, and particular activities you choose to partake in. Each season has its distinct charms, and organizing your vacation based on these aspects may assure a memorable and gratifying stay in this magnificent country.

Visa Requirements

If you are going to visit Namibia, you may require a visa depending on your nationality. According to the Namibian Ministry of Home Affairs, Immigration, Safety and Security, travelers from more than 50 countries do not need visas for up to 90 days.

However, you must have a valid passport that is at least six months beyond your intended departure date and have adequate pages for entrance and exit stamps (at least three blank pages). If you are not from a visa-exempt country, you may apply for a visa on arrival at Hosea Kutako International Airport in Windhoek for N$1200 (approximately $80 USD) or in advance via a Namibian consulate or embassy in your country.

You will need to show proof of adequate finances, travel papers, and a completed application form[1]. If you are traveling with children under 18, you must additionally carry a certified copy of each child's original birth certificate and a certified permission from the other parent if traveling with just one parent.

Countries Exempted From a Visa

Namibia has a visa exemption agreement with more than 50 countries, indicating that travelers from those countries do not require a visa to enter Namibia for up to 90 days. Some of the countries that are exempted from obtaining a visa to enter Namibia include:

- Angola, Australia, Austria, Belgium, Botswana, Brazil, Canada, Cuba, Denmark, Finland, France, Germany, Hong Kong, Iceland, Ireland, Italy, Japan, Kazakhstan, Kenya, Kyrgyzstan, Lesotho, Liechtenstein, Luxembourg, Macau SAR, Malawi, Malaysia, Mauritius, Moldova, Mozambique, Netherlands, New Zealand, Norway, Portugal, Russia and the CIS, Rwanda, Seychelles, Singapore, South Africa, Spain, Swaziland, Sweden, Switzerland, Tajikistan, Tanzania, Turkmenistan, Ukraine, United Kingdom (including all classes of British nationality), United States of America (including American Samoa), Uzbekistan and Zambia.

- Holders of diplomatic or official passports from Ghana, Congo (Brazzaville), India and Venezuela are also free from having a visa to visit Namibia.

- African bearers of diplomatic or official passports are free from Namibian visas.

You may discover the comprehensive list of visa-exempt countries on the Namibian Ministry of Home Affairs website. Please note that the list may vary from time to time and it is suggested that you check your visa needs before flying to Namibia.

Choosing Your Itinerary

When arranging your itinerary for Namibia, consider the following considerations to make the most of your visit:

Duration of Stay: Determine how much time you have available for your vacation. Namibia is a huge country with numerous sights, so plan your schedule depending on the amount of days you can spend exploring.

Must-Visit Destinations: Identify the must-visit locations or attractions that interest you the most.

Popular sites include Etosha National Park for animals, the Namib Desert for famous dunes, Swakopmund for coastal experiences, and Sossusvlei for spectacular views.

Travel hobbies: Consider your travel hobbies and preferences. If you appreciate animals, concentrate on safari excursions in national parks. For adventure lovers, opt for activities like dune boarding, quad biking, or hiking. If you're a photography aficionado, schedule your visit for the finest lighting conditions.

Season and Weather: Be cautious of the time of year you intend to come. Each season provides distinct experiences, whether it's viewing the desert blossom after showers, enjoying warm temperatures during the dry season, or observing migratory bird arrivals.

Travel Logistics: Plan your route and logistics carefully. Some sites in Namibia may need lengthier journey hours, so consider closeness while building your schedule to prevent wasteful driving.

Local Culture and Communities: Include trips to local communities or cultural events to immerse yourself in Namibia's rich history and customs. Community-based tourism projects may give insights into the local way of life.

Accommodation and Reservations: Book lodgings in advance, particularly if you're going during the high season or peak tourist times. This guarantees you have a place to stay and enables you to organize your trip around your lodgings.

Particular tastes: Customize your itinerary depending on your particular tastes and travel style. Whether you like a calm pace, an energetic adventure, or a combination of both, adapt your plans to meet your interests.

Remember to allow some flexibility in your schedule for unplanned discoveries or adjustments to your plans. Namibia's wide landscapes and natural beauties may present unexpected chances, and being open to spontaneity may improve your entire travel experience. Happy planning and enjoy your amazing tour across Namibia!

Health and Safety Tips

When going to Namibia, it's vital to take health and safety measures to guarantee a safe and pleasurable journey. Here are some health and safety considerations for your visit:

Vaccinations and Health Precautions:
- Check with a healthcare expert or travel clinic to establish the needed immunisations and health precautions for Namibia. Common immunisations may include hepatitis A, typhoid, tetanus, and yellow fever (needed if arriving from a yellow fever endemic region).
- Consider taking malaria prophylaxis if you intend to travel places with a risk of malaria transmission. Consult your doctor for the most recommended prescription depending on your health and travel plan.

Drinking Water:
- Drink bottled or boiling water in Namibia. Avoid eating tap water or beverages with ice from questionable sources to avoid waterborne infections.

Sun Protection:
- Namibia has significant amounts of solar exposure. Protect yourself against sunburn and heatstroke by wearing sunscreen with a high SPF, a wide-brimmed hat, sunglasses, and lightweight, loose-fitting clothes.

Wildlife Safety:
- Observe nature from a safe distance and never approach or provoke animals. Follow the rules issued by park rangers during wildlife drives and walks to guarantee your safety and respect for the animals' environment.

Road Safety:
- If self-driving, be careful on the roads, particularly in rural regions. Watch out for animals crossing the roads, and drive at safe speeds, since some roads may have loose gravel or sand.
- Carry adequate water and supplies while going to rural places, since services may be restricted.

Crime Prevention:
- Namibia is quite secure for travelers, but it's vital to take common-sense measures. Avoid exhibiting costly products or carrying big quantities of cash. Keep your valuables safe and remain cautious in busy settings.

Hygiene:
- Practice proper hygiene, particularly frequent handwashing, to lower the risk of sickness.

Travel Insurance:
- Purchase comprehensive travel insurance that covers medical emergencies, trip cancellations, and evacuation if required.

Emergency Information:
- Save emergency contact numbers, including the local emergency services and your country's embassy or consulate in Namibia.

Respect Local Customs:
- Respect local norms and traditions, including clothing regulations and photography prohibitions, particularly in culturally sensitive regions.

By following these health and safety precautions, you may help guarantee a pleasant and worry-free tour across Namibia, enabling you to completely experience the beauty and adventure the country has to offer.

Safety in National Parks and Wilderness Areas

Safety in Namibia's national parks and wilderness regions is vital to provide a happy and secure animal and nature experience. While these regions provide wonderful chances for exploration and animal interactions, visitors should be mindful of possible hazards and take essential measures. Here are some safety considerations when visiting national parks and wilderness regions in Namibia:

Park Regulations and Guidelines: Familiarize oneself with the park's regulations and procedures before visiting. Follow directions from park rangers and stick to defined areas for visitors' safety and the protection of animals.

Wildlife Viewing: Always keep a safe distance from animals. Observe animals from a distance, and never approach or provoke them. Use binoculars or zoom lenses for close-ups.

Stay on Marked Trails: Stick to authorized trails and routes when hiking or exploring. Venturing off-trail may be perilous and may destroy delicate ecosystems.

Travel in Groups: Traveling in groups is safer than traveling alone, particularly when visiting distant or less-visited locations. Inform someone reputable about your vacation intentions and planned return time.

Inform Rangers of Your Plans: When departing on treks or prolonged trips, advise park rangers of your route and estimated return time. This enables them to react rapidly in case of emergency.

Carry Sufficient Water and Supplies: Bring adequate water and food, particularly if you intend to explore locations without easy access to facilities. Be prepared for rapid weather changes.

Vehicle Safety: When traveling through national parks, remain on approved routes and respect speed restrictions. Watch carefully for animals crossing the roadways, particularly between dawn and twilight.

Respect Wildlife and Their Habitat: Avoid upsetting animals or their natural habitats. Do not feed animals, since it might affect their behavior and impair their health.

First Aid Kit with Emergency Supplies: Carry a basic first aid kit and emergency supplies, including a charged cell phone with emergency contacts recorded.

Be Prepared for Limited Connectivity: National parks and wilderness regions may have limited or no cellphone coverage. Be prepared to be out of communication throughout your stay.

By respecting these safety recommendations, you may have a memorable and secure vacation while interacting with Namibia's magnificent wildlife and natural treasures.

Remember that safety is a shared responsibility, and being conscious of your surroundings helps preserve both yourself and the varied ecosystems you meet.

Useful Websites and Apps

When going to Namibia, there are various handy websites and applications that may improve your experience and give crucial information. Here are some suggested ones:

Websites:

Namibia Tourism Board: The official website of the Namibia Tourism Board offers extensive information on attractions, lodgings, activities, and travel guides for travelers visiting Namibia. (Website: https://www.namibiatourism.com.na/)

Etosha National Park: The official website of Etosha National Park contains facts about the park's animals, hotels, and tourist requirements. (Website: https://www.etoshanationalpark.org/)

Tracks4Africa: This website provides comprehensive maps and GPS data for self-drive adventures in Namibia and other African countries. (Website: https://tracks4africa.co.za/)

iOverlander: A crowd-sourced app and website that gives information about campsites, motels, and other travel-related data, valuable for road trips and outdoor experiences. (Website: https://ioverlander.com/)

Kruger Sightings: Although Kruger Sightings largely focuses on South Africa's Kruger National Park, many visitors visit both Namibia and South Africa on the same trip. This software enables users to share wildlife observations and follow animal movements in real-time. (Website: https://www.krugerpark.co.za/)

Apps:

Maps.Me: An offline map tool that enables you to download maps of Namibia and navigate without an internet connection. (Available for iOS and Android)

Currency Converter Plus: An app that lets you convert Namibian Dollars to your local currency and vice versa. (Available for iOS and Android)

Namibian Weather: A weather app that gives predictions for several places in Namibia, useful for planning outdoor activities. (Available for iOS and Android)

XE Currency: A reputable currency converter tool that enables conversions for Namibian Dollars and other currencies. (Available for iOS and Android)

Google Translate: Useful for interpreting phrases and connecting with locals, since Namibia contains various indigenous languages. (Available for iOS and Android)

Remember to download any essential applications and offline maps before your trip to ensure they are available throughout your travels, particularly if you intend to journey into more distant places with poor internet availability. Additionally, always check for the most up-to-date information and user reviews for applications before downloading them on your smartphone.

Fun Facts:

Namibia is a photographer's dream, delivering stunning vistas, brilliant sunsets, and exciting animal encounters that will leave any nature lover in wonder.

GETTING AROUND NAMIBIA

Transportation Options

When visiting Namibia, numerous transportation choices are available to discover the country's different landscapes and attractions. Here are some popular transit choices:

Domestic Flights

Domestic flights in Namibia provide a practical and time-efficient option to travel between various parts of the country, given the huge distances and varied scenery. The projected prices for domestic flights in Namibia might vary based on the airline, route, and time of booking. Here are some crucial facts to know regarding domestic flights, along with estimated costs:

Airlines and Airports: Air Namibia conducts regular flights between major cities including Windhoek, Walvis Bay, Ondangwa, and Katima Mulilo. Kulula, a private airline, operates flights linking Windhoek, Walvis Bay, and Lüderitz.

Flights run from the principal international airport, Hosea Kutako International Airport (WDH), situated approximately 45 kilometers east of Windhoek, and Eros Airport (ERS) in Windhoek.

Flight Routes: Domestic flights link major cities, villages, and tourist spots, making it simpler to visit national parks, coastal areas, and other isolated locations. Estimated expenses for one-way domestic flights inside Namibia vary from $100 to $300, depending on the route and distance.

Frequency and Timings: The frequency of domestic flights may vary depending on demand and the season, with more frequent flights during high tourist seasons. It's best to book flights in advance to receive cheaper fares. Last-minute reservations may be more costly.

Luggage Allowance: Check with the airline for their luggage allotment and limitations, since each airline may have different regulations regarding baggage weight and size constraints.

Flight Duration: Flight durations in Namibia might vary based on the distance and destination. Flights between large cities are quite short, typically approximately one hour.

Booking Tickets: Domestic flight tickets may be ordered via the airlines' official websites, travel agents, or at airport ticket counters.

Scenic Flights: Some airlines provide beautiful flights over notable Namibian landscapes, such as the Sossusvlei dunes or the Skeleton Coast. These beautiful flights give unique aerial views of the country's magnificent splendor.

The projected cost for scenic flights may vary from $150 to $500, depending on the time and location.
Using domestic flights in Namibia may save time and enable you to travel big distances swiftly, optimizing your time for exploration and appreciating the many attractions the country has to offer. Remember that rates are subject to change, so it's best to check with the airlines directly for the most up-to-date charges.

Self-Drive vs. Guided Tours

Self-Drive:

Cost: Renting a vehicle for self-drive gives flexibility and freedom to explore Namibia at your own speed. The typical cost of hiring a standard sedan automobile begins at $50 to $100 each day, depending on the rental operator, kind of vehicle, and length of the rental.

Fuel: Fuel rates in Namibia are quite low, with gasoline prices averaging approximately $1 per liter.

The amount spent on gasoline will depend on your journey distance and the fuel efficiency of the car.

Accommodation: Self-drive enables you to pick accommodation depending on your budget and preferences. Accommodation expenses vary based on the kind of housing, ranging from inexpensive guest houses at $30 to $100 per night to luxury lodges at $200 to $500 per night.

Food: The cost of food in Namibia varies, with affordable meals at local restaurants or street sellers costing from $5 to $15 each meal. Fine dining at upmarket places may run from $30 to $60 per person for lunch.

Park prices: National park admission prices per person vary, with rates for international visitors ranging from $5 to $20 per day, depending on the location and activities. Vehicle admission costs are supplementary, generally ranging from $10 to $50 per day.

Guided Tours:

Cost: Guided tours provide convenience and professional knowledge, but they come at a greater price than self-drive. The cost of guided tours varies on the itinerary, length, party size, and degree of luxury.

A guided tour package may cost from $200 to $500 or more per person each day.

Inclusions: Guided tours generally include hotel, food, park fees, and activities in their package rates, giving an all-inclusive experience.

Group vs. Private Tours: Group excursions are more economical, but you'll be traveling with other people. Private excursions provide a customized experience but come with higher fees.

Expert Guides: Guided excursions often come with expert guides that give great insights into the sites, wildlife, and cultural elements of Namibia.

Consider your travel tastes, budget, and the sort of experience you wish to have when picking between self-drive and guided tours. Self-drive gives you freedom and expense management, while guided excursions provide convenience and access to professional expertise. Both alternatives provide unique opportunities to discover the stunning scenery and animals of Namibia. Remember to verify with tour operators for exact package items and prices to make an educated selection.

Public Transport

Public transport in Namibia is offered in the form of buses and minibuses, giving a cheap alternative for commuting between towns and cities. However, it's vital to highlight that public transit is less frequent and less developed compared to private transportation choices. Here's an overview of public transit in Namibia:

Inter-City Buses:
- Inter-city buses travel between major towns and cities in Namibia, linking different parts of the country.
- These buses are a cost-effective choice for long-distance travel, with ticket rates ranging based on the route and the operator.
- While intercity buses are available, their timetables may not be as regular as in more urbanized regions, so it's vital to plan your travel in advance.

Minibuses and Shared Taxis:
- Minibuses and shared taxis are widespread types of public transport, particularly for shorter excursions inside cities or between towns.
- Minibuses are known as "combis" and are a common form of transportation for residents and visitors alike.

- Shared taxis may not have defined timetables, and they normally leave when full, therefore they might be less reliable in terms of departure timings.

Rural Routes:
- Public transport alternatives may be restricted in rural locations, when travel between smaller communities could be less frequent.
- In such instances, it's vital to plan your journey ahead of time and be prepared for extended waiting periods or seek alternate transit choices.

Connectivity:
- While public transit connects major towns and cities, be aware that certain isolated places and tourist destinations may not have direct public transport access.
- For these places, you may need to explore different transportation choices, such as hiring a vehicle or joining guided excursions.

Safety and Comfort:
- Public transport in Namibia is typically secure, but it's vital to be attentive about your valuables and personal safety, particularly in packed cars.

- Minibuses may become extremely full, and drivers may drive rapidly, therefore it's vital to find trustworthy operators and emphasize safety.

Public transport may be a cost-effective method to discover Namibia and engage with people. However, it may involve more organization and flexibility compared to private transportation choices like hiring a vehicle or attending guided excursions. Consider your schedule, travel preferences, and budget when choosing the best form of transport for your Namibian vacation.

Where to Renting a Vehicle

In Namibia, you may hire automobiles from several rental organizations, including international car rental corporations and local ones. Here are some frequent venues where you may hire a car in Namibia:

Hosea Kutako International Airport (Windhoek): Many international and local automobile rental firms operate counters at Hosea Kutako International Airport (HKIA), which is the principal international airport in Namibia. Renting a vehicle right at the airport upon arrival provides convenience for passengers.

Eros Airport (Windhoek): Eros Airport is a small airport in Windhoek, and certain car rental firms may have offices or offer airport shuttle services for vehicle pickup and drop-off.

Downtown Windhoek and Other Cities: Car rental firms have offices in the downtown sections of large cities including Windhoek, Swakopmund, Walvis Bay, and other metropolitan locations. You may visit these offices to hire a car.

Online Booking: Many automobile rental businesses in Namibia feature online booking options, enabling you to reserve a vehicle in advance and secure your desired vehicle type.

Travel Agencies and Tour Operators: Some travel firms and tour operators in Namibia may also provide automobile rental services as part of their trip packages.
When hiring a car in Namibia, it's vital to examine aspects such as the kind of vehicle, rental fees, insurance coverage, and rental terms and conditions. Ensure that you have a valid driver's license and any extra paperwork requested by the rental business. Additionally, thoroughly read and understand the rental agreement before signing to prevent any misunderstandings during your rental duration.

Comparing prices and services from multiple rental firms will help you get the best bargain for your requirements and preferences. Whether you want to tour Namibia's national parks, desert landscapes, or coastal places, renting a car provides the freedom and flexibility to appreciate the country's many attractions at your own leisure.

Road Conditions and Regulations

Road conditions and laws in Namibia might vary based on the kind of road and the location you are driving through. Here are some crucial aspects to know about road conditions and rules in Namibia:

Road Conditions: Namibia features a blend of paved and dirt roads. Major highways and roads linking key cities are typically well-maintained and paved, delivering enjoyable driving experiences.
In more isolated places, notably in national parks and rural districts, you may find gravel or dirt roads, which may be difficult and demand cautious driving, especially during the rainy season when roads may become slick.
Be aware of potholes and rapid changes in road conditions, particularly in rural regions.

4x4 Vehicles: Some locations, such as the Namib Desert and portions of Damaraland, need 4x4 vehicles for entry owing to the hard terrain.

If you want to visit off-the-beaten-path sites, consider hiring a 4x4 vehicle to guarantee you can reach these regions securely.

Speed Limits and Driving Regulations: Speed restrictions are severely enforced in Namibia. The typical speed limit on open highways is 120 km/h (approximately 75 mph), although it may change in particular regions, therefore look for posted signs.
Seat belts are essential for all persons in the car, and the use of mobile phones while driving is forbidden unless using a hands-free device.

Wildlife on Roads: Be aware of animals on the roadways, particularly in national parks and rural regions. Animals, such as antelope, warthogs, and even bigger animals like elephants, may cross the road unexpectedly. Drive gently and be prepared to stop if required.

Roadside Assistance: Namibia offers limited roadside assistance services in certain locations, so it's vital to be self-sufficient and carry basic supplies like water, a spare tire, and a first aid kit.
Fuel Stations:

Fuel stations are present in large towns and along significant routes.

However, it's best to top up your tank before beginning on extended travels, particularly in more rural places.

Night Driving: Driving at night in Namibia may be perilous, particularly on remote roads. Many incidents include animal interactions at night, therefore it's best to restrict night driving if possible.

Border Crossing: If you want to go to adjacent countries from Namibia by car, be sure to verify the unique border crossing rules and restrictions for each country.

By complying to traffic restrictions, driving cautiously, and being prepared for varied road conditions, you may have a safe and happy driving experience while experiencing the stunning landscapes of Namibia. Remember that road conditions may vary depending on weather and maintenance, so keep informed and plan your journeys appropriately.

NAMIBIA'S TOP DESTINATIONS

Windhoek

Windhoek is the capital and biggest city of Namibia, located in the middle section of the country. It serves as the political, economic, and cultural heart of Namibia, providing a blend of contemporary facilities and colonial beauty. Here are some important features of Windhoek:

Independence Avenue: Independence Avenue is the major thoroughfare in Windhoek and the hub of the city's business and retail sector. It's dotted with restaurants, stores, and cafés, making it a popular place for both residents and visitors.

Christuskirche (Christ Church): This historic Lutheran church, erected during the German colonial period, is one of the city's most identifiable structures. The neo-Gothic architectural style and the gorgeous grounds around the church make it a popular destination for photography.

Tintenpalast (Ink Palace): The Tintenpalast is the seat of Namibia's parliament, situated in the city center. Visitors may join guided tours to learn about the country's political history and the operation of its government.

National Museum of Namibia: The National Museum features exhibitions on Namibia's history, culture, and natural heritage. It gives insight into the country's varied ethnic groups, historic relics, and the battle for freedom.

Craft Markets and Street Markets: Windhoek offers various craft markets and street markets where tourists may purchase traditional crafts, jewelry, fabrics, and souvenirs. The Post Street Mall and the Namibia Craft Centre are popular destinations for shopping.

Heroes' Acre: Located close outside Windhoek, Heroes' Acre is a national monument and burial ground honoring Namibia's heroes and heroines who fought for freedom. The position provides panoramic views of the city and adjacent countryside.

Zoo Park: The Zoo Park is a green park in the city center, excellent for resting, walking, and enjoying the outdoors. It's a favorite area for folks to relax over weekends.

Restaurants and Cuisine: Windhoek provides a rich culinary scene with restaurants presenting a mix of local Namibian cuisine, as well as foreign specialties. Don't miss the chance to enjoy local delicacies like game meat and biltong.

Cultural Events and Festivals: Throughout the year, Windhoek holds many cultural events, art exhibits, and festivals, allowing tourists an opportunity to experience Namibian music, dancing, and arts.

Windhoek's blend of contemporary metropolitan facilities and historic charm gives a good starting point for seeing the remainder of Namibia's beautiful landscapes and natural treasures. The city's central position also makes it a suitable base for tourists to start their experiences in this lovely African country.

Sossusvlei and Namib-Naukluft National Park

Sossusvlei and Namib-Naukluft National Park are two prominent and stunning sites situated in the southern section of Namibia. They are part of the Namib Desert, one of the oldest and most dry deserts in the world. Here's all you need to know about these fascinating places:

Sossusvlei: Sossusvlei is a clay and salt pan surrounded by towering red sand dunes, some of which reach heights of over 300 meters (almost 1000 ft). It is one of Namibia's most renowned and photographed natural attractions.

The term "Sossusvlei" means "dead-end marsh" in the local Nama language, alluding to the fact that the Tsauchab River, which periodically runs through the region, seldom reaches the vlei (pan) itself.

The contrasting hues of the red sand dunes against the white clay pans and blue sky make a spectacular and surreal picture, especially around dawn and sunset.

Deadvlei: Adjacent to Sossusvlei lies Deadvlei, a clay pit littered with dead acacia trees. The sharp contrast between the charred trees and the surrounding white pan and red dunes makes Deadvlei a popular shooting destination.

Dune 45: Dune 45 is one of the most photographed sand dunes in Namibia. Visitors typically climb it early in the morning to observe the sunrise and enjoy amazing views of the surrounding desert.

Namib-Naukluft National Park: Sossusvlei and Deadvlei are part of the broader Namib-Naukluft National Park, which encompasses an area of roughly 50,000 square kilometers (about 19,000 square miles) and is one of Africa's biggest national parks.

The park's various features include towering sand dunes, wide gravel plains, harsh mountains, and the remarkable

Sesriem Canyon, which was created by the Tsauchab River.

Activities: The major activities at Sossusvlei and Namib-Naukluft National Park are hiking, photography, and enjoying the unique desert environment.

Climbing the sand dunes, visiting Deadvlei and Sossusvlei, and trekking through the Sesriem Canyon are popular activities for tourists.

Best Time to Visit: The best time to visit Sossusvlei and Namib-Naukluft National Park is during the colder months from April to October when temperatures are more mild for outdoor activities.

However, going during the warmer months from November to March affords an opportunity to view the desert's amazing wildlife, including oryx, springbok, and desert-adapted elephants.

Conservation: Namib-Naukluft National Park is committed to protecting the sensitive desert ecology and its distinctive flora and animals. Visitors are asked to observe park laws and guidelines to minimize their influence on the ecosystem.

Sossusvlei and Namib-Naukluft National Park provide a genuinely surreal experience, enabling visitors to immerse themselves in the immensity and magnificence of the Namib Desert. Whether you're an explorer, photographer, or nature lover, this unique location offers an extraordinary tour through some of the world's most breathtaking landscapes.

Etosha National Park

Etosha National Park is one of Namibia's most recognised and known national parks, situated in the northwestern region of the country. It is recognised for its enormous salt pan, rich fauna, and unusual sceneries. Here's everything you need to know about Etosha National Park:

Etosha Pan: The park's showpiece is the Etosha Pan, a huge, flat, white expanse of salt that can be seen from space. The pan is dry for most of the year, but during the rainy season, it occasionally contains shallow water, attracting a diversity of species.

Abundant Wildlife: Etosha is home to a varied diversity of animals, including elephants, lions, rhinos, giraffes, zebras, and other antelope species. The park's dry nature makes animal viewing reasonably simple, particularly near waterholes.

Waterholes and Game Viewing: Etosha has various natural and manmade waterholes dotted across the area.

These waterholes are ideal sites for seeing wildlife, since animals flock here to drink and cool off.

Game drives, both self-directed and guided, are popular methods to explore the park and watch its animals.

Self-Drive Game Viewing: Etosha is known for its superb self-drive game watching chances. The park's well-maintained gravel roads let tourists reach different locations, waterholes, and viewpoint spots at their own time.

Accommodation: Etosha provides different lodging alternatives, including rest camps, lodges, and private game reserves both within and beyond the park limits. Accommodation varies from simple camping sites to upscale resorts.

Birdwatching: Etosha is also a sanctuary for birdwatchers, with over 300 bird species reported in the park. The pan draws migrating birds during the wet season, making it an ideal place for birding.

Etosha Pan and Salt Pans:

The Etosha Pan and its adjoining salt pans provide a unique and spectacular environment. The vast, flat plain reaches to the horizon, affording magnificent picture opportunities, particularly around dawn and sunset.

Park Gates and Entrance Fees: Etosha has multiple entrance gates, including Anderson Gate, Von Lindequist Gate, Galton Gate, and King Nehale Gate. Entrance costs for the park vary for international visitors and are valid for a set number of days.

Etosha in Different Seasons: The best time to visit Etosha for wildlife watching is during the dry season (May to October) when animals concentrate near waterholes. The wet season (November to April) is wonderful for birding and observing the vegetation.

Etosha National Park provides a memorable safari experience with its great animal sightings and captivating sceneries. Whether you're a wildlife enthusiast, photographer, or nature lover, a visit to Etosha guarantees a genuine and exciting African safari encounter.

Damaraland

Damaraland is a mountainous and lonely area situated in the northern section of Namibia. It is recognised for its spectacular scenery, distinctive geological formations, ancient rock art, and desert-adapted animals. Here's an outline of Damaraland and its significant highlights:

Geological Marvels: Damaraland is distinguished by stunning rock formations, granite mountains, and huge plains.
The region's historic volcanic mountains, such as the Brandberg Mountain, form a spectacular background for exploration.

Twyfelfontein Rock Engravings: Twyfelfontein is a UNESCO World Heritage Site noted for its prehistoric rock carvings and rock paintings. These engravings, produced by the San people thousands of years ago, represent animals, human figures, and abstract patterns.

Petrified Forest: The Petrified Forest, situated near the village of Khorixas, is a remarkable attraction with petrified tree trunks that are believed to be about 280 million years old. The petrified trees are relics of a beautiful forest that thrived in the region long ago.

Desert-Adapted Wildlife: Damaraland is home to a unique assortment of desert-adapted animals, including desert-adapted elephants, desert lions, and the endangered black rhino. These creatures have acquired particular adaptations to thrive in the dry environment.

Twyfelfontein Adventure Camp: For tourists seeking an unforgettable experience in the heart of Damaraland, the Twyfelfontein Adventure Camp provides an opportunity to interact with nature while enjoying excellent lodgings.

Organ Pipes and Burnt Mountain: The Organ Pipes are a geological structure of dolerite columns that resemble a gigantic pipe organ. Nearby, the Burnt Mountain shows colorful rocks caused by volcanic action millions of years ago.

Cultural Encounters: Damaraland provides chances to connect with local populations, such as the Damara people, to learn about their rituals, traditions, and distinctive way of life.

Wildlife Conservation: Several conservancies in Damaraland concentrate on animal conservation and community-based tourism. Visiting these conservancies promotes conservation efforts and gives a genuine cultural experience.

Scenic Drives and Hiking: Damaraland is a delight for nature lovers and trekkers. Scenic drives and hiking routes enable tourists to experience the area's stunning scenery and see its animals up close.

Damaraland's rugged beauty and distinctive attractions make it an off-the-beaten-path location, suitable for those seeking a deeper connection with nature and culture. The region's austere but intriguing nature, mixed with its rich history and teeming wildlife, produces an amazing tour across one of Namibia's most spectacular environments.

Caprivi Strip

The Caprivi Strip, also known as the Zambezi Region, is a short strip of territory situated in the northeastern section of Namibia. It is a distinctive and distinct location, defined by its lush green scenery, many rivers, and diversified species. Here's an overview of the Caprivi Strip and its significant highlights:

Location & Geography: The Caprivi Strip is a panhandle-shaped territory that runs roughly 450 kilometers (280 miles) from the northeastern tip of Namibia to the Zambezi River. It is surrounded by Angola to the north, Zambia to the east, and Botswana to the south.

Rivers and Waterways: The Caprivi Strip is traversed by numerous large rivers, including the Zambezi, Chobe, Kwando (also known as the Linyanti), and Okavango. These streams produce a distinct and lush ecology that contrasts with the desert landscapes seen in other regions of Namibia.

Bwabwata National Park: Bwabwata National Park is one of the biggest protected areas in the Caprivi Strip, comprising a wide area of different ecosystems. The park is recognised for its diverse wildlife, including elephants, buffalo, antelopes, and different bird species.

Mahango Game Reserve: Another significant wildlife reserve is Mahango Game Reserve, which is situated in the eastern part of the Caprivi Strip. It provides good chances for game viewing and birding.

Water-Based Activities: The variety of rivers and canals in the Caprivi Strip provides for different water-based activities, such as boat safaris, fishing, and canoeing. These activities provide a unique approach to enjoy the region's natural splendor and watch animals along the riverbanks.

Cultural Heritage: The Caprivi Strip is home to various ethnic groups, including the San, Lozi, and Subia people. Visitors get the chance to learn about their ancient rituals, dancing, and crafts.

Katima Mulilo: Katima Mulilo is the biggest town and capital of the Zambezi Region. It serves as the principal economic and administrative hub of the Caprivi Strip.

Access to Other Countries: The Caprivi Strip offers a crucial land corridor linking Namibia to other Southern

African countries, notably Zambia, Zimbabwe, and Botswana. This strategic placement makes it a key transit route in the area.

The Caprivi Strip's unusual physical characteristics, diversified fauna, and cultural diversity make it a desirable location for those seeking an off-the-beaten-path experience in Namibia. Whether you're interested in animal encounters, water-based activities, or cultural immersion, the Caprivi Strip provides a thrilling and unique tour through this beautiful and colorful area.

Fish River Canyon

Fish River Canyon is one of Namibia's most beautiful natural marvels and a must-visit location for those traveling the southern section of the country. It is the second-largest canyon in the world, behind the Grand Canyon in the United States. Here's an overview of Fish River Canyon and its significant highlights:

Size and Location: Fish River Canyon covers around 160 kilometers (100 miles) in length, with depths reaching up to 550 meters (1,800 feet) and widths of up to 27 kilometers (17 miles).
The canyon is situated in the southernmost portion of Namibia, near to the border with South Africa.

Geological Formation: The canyon was built over millions of years by erosion by the Fish River, which is one of Namibia's longest rivers. The river's slow but steady flow eroded its way through the stony environment, producing the spectacular canyon we see today.

Hiking Trails: One of the most popular activities in Fish River Canyon is the Fish River Canyon Hiking Trail. This tough multi-day walk leads hikers through the canyon bottom, giving stunning vistas and interactions with unusual flora and animals.
The hiking season normally spans from May through September when the temperature is cooler.

Scenic Viewpoints: There are various overlooks around the lip of the canyon that give beautiful panoramic views of the rocky scenery and the flowing Fish River below. The prominent perspectives are the prominent Viewpoint, Hells Bend, and the Ai-Ais Hot Springs viewpoint.

Wildlife: While the canyon itself is very barren, the surrounding plains and riverbed are home to a variety of desert-adapted fauna, including kudu, mountain zebra, and baboons.

Birdwatchers may also see a number of bird species, including raptors and other desert-loving birds.

Ai-Ais Hot Springs Resort: The Ai-Ais Hot Springs Resort is situated at the southern end of the canyon and is noted for its natural hot springs. It provides a soothing halt for travelers after a tough walk or a day of exploring.

Conservation: Fish River Canyon and its surrounding surroundings are protected as part of the Ai-Ais/Richtersveld Transfrontier Park, a transboundary conservation area shared by Namibia and South Africa.

Fish River Canyon's rough beauty and unusual geological characteristics make it an outstanding location for nature enthusiasts, hikers, and photographers. The awe-inspiring sights and the sensation of seclusion among the grandeur of the canyon make a memorable and introspective experience for tourists experiencing this natural marvel in Namibia.

Fun Facts:

Namibia features one of Africa's most diversified and unusual animal populations, including the uncommon desert-adapted elephants and the endangered black rhinos. Etosha National Park provides fantastic opportunities for animal safaris.

WHERE TO STAY

Budget Accommodations

There are several possibilities for affordable hotels, lodges and self-catering flats in Namibia. These are some of the top-rated ones you should consider:

Beach Lodge Swakopmund

- **Location**: Swakopmund, on the Atlantic coast of Namibia
- **Charges:** From $75 per night for a double room with sea view
- **Services**: Free internet, breakfast included, restaurant, bar, surfer's corner
- **Highlights**: Child-friendly, fantastic service, kind welcome, magnificent views

Ndhovu Safari Lodge

- **Location**: Mahango Game Reserve, along the Okavango River
- **Charges**: From $100 per night for a tented cabin with ensuite bathroom
- **Services**: Free internet, breakfast included, pool, bar, laundry service
- **Highlights**: Gracious host, nice staff, wildlife watching, river cruise

Hotel Thule

- **Location:** Windhoek, the capital city of Namibia Charges: From $120 per night for a basic room with city view
- **Services:** Free internet, breakfast included, restaurant, bar, pool, gym, spa
- **Highlights**: Beautiful view of the city, lovely terrace, pleasant rooms, friendly staff

Hohenstein Lodge

- **Location**: Erongo Mountains, near the Spitzkoppe rock formation
- **Charges**: From $130 per night for a bungalow with mountain view
- **Services**: Free internet, breakfast included, restaurant, bar, pool
- **Highlights**: Easy to locate, beautifully decorated rooms, amazing view of Hohenstein mountain

Aloegrove Safari Lodge

- **Location**: Otjiwarongo, near the Waterberg Plateau Park Charges: From $140 per night for a chalet with ensuite bathroom
- **Services:** Free wifi, breakfast included, restaurant, bar, pool
- **Highlights**: Beautiful location on a hill, nice food, big range of animals, feeding of big cats

Mid Range Accommodations

There are numerous possibilities for pleasant and reasonable hotels, lodges and guesthouses in Namibia. Here are some of the top-rated ones based on the ratings and costs:

Gabus Game Ranch Safari Lodge
- **Location:** Otavi, near the Uisib Mountain
- **Charges**: From $100 per night for a double accommodation with garden view
- **Services**: Free internet, breakfast included, restaurant, bar, outdoor pool, laundry service
- **Highlights**: Modern and spacious accommodations, views of the nearby waterhole, home-style cooking, wildlife drives, hiking, bird watching

Safarihoek Lodge
- **Location:** Kamanjab, outside the south-western boundary of Etosha National Park
- **Charges**: From $200 per night for a chalet with ensuite bathroom
- **Services**: Free internet, breakfast included, restaurant, bar, pool
- **Highlights**: Air-conditioned accommodations, panoramic views of Etosha, solar-powered resort, animal watching

Windhoek Country Club Resort
- **Location**: Windhoek, the capital city of Namibia
  Charges: From $150 per night for a medium room with garden view
- **Services**: Free internet, breakfast included, restaurant, bar, pool, gym, spa, casino
- **Highlights**: Elegant accommodations, nice staff, golf course, entertainment choices

Swakopmund Guesthouse
- **Location**: Swakopmund, on the Atlantic coast of Namibia
- **Charges**: From $120 per night for a double room with garden view
- **Services**: Free internet, breakfast included, laundry service
- **Highlights**: Stylish and spacious accommodations, strategic location, helpful staff

Etosha Safari Camp
- **Location**: Etosha South, near the Anderson Gate of Etosha National Park
- **Charges**: From $90 per night for a double room with ensuite bathroom
- **Services**: Free internet, breakfast included, restaurant, bar, pool

- **Highlights**: Funky and colorful rooms, exciting atmosphere, game drives

Luxurious Options

There are numerous possibilities for spectacular and premium hotels, resorts and camps in Namibia. Here are some of the top ones based on reviews and costs:

Beyond Sossusvlei Desert Lodge
- **Location**: NamibRand Nature Reserve, near the Sossusvlei dunes
- **Charges**: From $1000 per night for a desert suite with ensuite bathroom
- **Services:** Free wifi, breakfast included, restaurant, bar, pool, spa, observatory
- **Highlights**: Stunning desert views, elegant rooms with skylights, solar-powered lodge, desert activities, stargazing

Hoanib Skeleton Coast Camp by Wilderness Safaris
- **Location**: Palmwag Concession, near the Skeleton Coast **Charges**: From $900 per night for a tented unit with ensuite bathroom
- **Services**: Free wifi, breakfast included, restaurant, bar, pool
- **Highlights**: Remote location, stylish tents, wildlife viewing, scenic flights

Zannier Hotels Sonop
- **Location**: Karas Region, near the Fish River Canyon
- **Charges**: From $800 per night for a tented suite with ensuite bathroom
- **Services:** Free internet, breakfast included, restaurant, bar, pool, spa
- **Highlights**: Vintage-inspired tents, stunning views of the desert hills, gourmet cuisine, wellness treatments

Little Kulala Camp by Wilderness Safaris
- **Location**: Kulala Wilderness Reserve, near the Sossusvlei dunes
- **Charges:** From $700 per night for a thatched kulala with ensuite bathroom
- **Services**: Free wifi, breakfast included, restaurant, bar, pool
- **Highlights**: Spacious and airy rooms with rooftop beds, private plunge pools, desert activities

Damaraland Camp by Wilderness Safaris
- **Location**: Torra Conservancy, near the Brandberg Mountain
- **Charges:** From $600 per night for a tented accommodation with ensuite bathroom
- **Services**: Free internet, breakfast included, restaurant, bar
- **Highlights:** Eco-friendly camp, comfy tents with views of the valley, community engagement, desert-adapted animals.

NAMIBIAN CUISINE AND DINING EXPERIENCE

Must-Try Local Dishes

Namibia provides a distinct combination of tastes inspired by its different cultures and customs. Here are some must-try native meals while visiting Namibia:

Biltong: Biltong is a famous Namibian food made from dried and cured meat, generally beef or game meat. It's popular among residents and tourists alike, typically consumed as a fast and delicious protein-packed meal.

Potjiekos: Potjiekos is a classic stew prepared in a cast-iron pot over an open fire. It generally comprises a combination of meat (such as game meat or cattle), veggies, and spices. This hearty meal is a mainstay at social events and camping vacations.

Kapana: Kapana is a renowned street cuisine in Namibia, consisting of grilled or barbecued beef, commonly served with a combination of spices, salt, and chile. It's a tasty and budget-friendly alternative beloved by natives around the country.

Vetkoek: Vetkoek is a tasty fried bread dough that may be served as a sweet or savory meal. When savory, it's commonly packed with minced meat, cheese, or jam, while the sweet form is drizzled with syrup or honey.

Oshifima (Mahangu Porridge): Oshifima is a traditional porridge prepared from mahangu (pearl millet) flour. It is a staple cuisine for the Ovambo people in northern Namibia and is often eaten with meat or vegetable stew.

Mopane Worms: Mopane worms are a delicacy in Namibia and other Southern African countries. These huge caterpillars are dried and may be eaten as a crispy and protein-rich snack.

Oryx and Kudu Steaks: Namibia's game reserves are home to numerous wildlife, including oryx and kudu. Their flesh is thin and tasty, making oryx and kudu steaks a sought-after delicacy at many restaurants.

Game Meat: Namibia is noted for its superb game meat, including springbok, zebra, and ostrich. Various restaurants and resorts provide game meat meals, providing tourists a chance to enjoy distinct flavors.

Melktert (Milk Tart): Melktert is a classic South African dessert also popular in Namibia.
It consists of a sweet pastry crust filled with a creamy milk and cinnamon custard.

When visiting Namibia, don't miss the chance to sample these unique cuisine and immerse yourself in the country's gastronomic treasures. From substantial stews to rare game meats and distinctive street dishes, Namibia provides a fantastic voyage for your taste senses.

Recommended Restaurants and Cafes

If you are intending to visit Namibia, you may be thinking where to eat and drink throughout your stay. Here are some of the best restaurants and cafés in Namibia that you may try:

Joe's Beer House: This is a popular restaurant in Windhoek, the capital city of Namibia, where you can enjoy a range of cuisine, from burgers and steaks to game meat and seafood. The restaurant also features a vast assortment of beers, wines, and cocktails, as well as a vibrant environment with live music and entertainment. Joe's Beer House is open every day from 11:00 am until 11:00 at night.

NICE Restaurant & Bar: This is a fine dining restaurant in Windhoek that provides Namibian cuisine with a contemporary touch.

The menu contains meals such as ostrich carpaccio, springbok steak, and crocodile curry, as well as vegetarian and vegan alternatives. The restaurant also features a bar that serves wine tastings, drinks, and appetizers. NICE Restaurant & Bar is open from Monday to Saturday from 12:00 pm to 10:00 pm.

Sardinia Blue Olive: This is an Italian restaurant in Windhoek that provides excellent pizza, spaghetti, salads, and desserts. The restaurant employs fresh ingredients and handmade sauces to make tasty meals that will fulfill your demands. Sardinia Blue Olive also includes a deli where you can purchase cheese, bread, olive oil, and other things. The restaurant is open from Monday to Saturday from 8:00 am to 10:00 pm, and on Sundays from 8:00 am to 3:00 pm.

Xwama Cultural Village & Restaurant: This is a unique destination in Windhoek where you can enjoy the culture and food of the Ovambo people, one of the major ethnic groups in Namibia. The restaurant provides traditional delicacies such as mopane worms, mahangu porridge, and oshikundu (a fermented drink produced from millet). You may also enjoy cultural events, crafts, and activities in the village. Xwama Cultural Village &

Restaurant is open from Monday to Saturday from 9:00 am to 10:00 pm.

The Tug Restaurant: This is a seafood restaurant in Swakopmund, a seaside town in Namibia that is noted for its German colonial architecture and adventurous sports. The restaurant is built on a tugboat that overlooks the Atlantic Ocean, giving spectacular views and excellent fish. The menu includes items such as oysters, calamari, lobster, and fish. The Tug Restaurant is open every day from 12:00 pm until 10:00 pm.

Village Café: This is a quaint café in Swakopmund that provides breakfast, lunch, coffee, and cake. The café offers a distinctive atmosphere and a pleasant staff that will make you feel at home. The menu comprises items such as eggs benedict, chicken pie, burgers, and salads, as well as handcrafted cakes and pastries. Village Café is open every day from 7:30 am to 5:00 pm.

These are just a few of the numerous restaurants and cafés that you may discover in Namibia. Whether you are seeking local or foreign food, informal or sophisticated eating, or meat or vegetarian alternatives, you will undoubtedly find something that meets your taste and budget in this great country.

Eating Like a Local in Namibia

Eating like a native in Namibia enables you to enjoy the country's various culinary traditions and tastes.
Here are some recommendations to help you enjoy traditional Namibian food and eat like a local:

Try Local Street Food: Explore the local food booths and street sellers to enjoy traditional street meals like kapana (grilled meat), boerewors (spiced sausage), and vetkoek (fried bread dough).

Visit Local Markets: Visit local markets to explore a range of fresh vegetables, traditional ingredients, and handcrafted treats. You may also discover unique crafts and souvenirs while enjoying the colorful ambiance of the markets.

Sample Game Meat: Embrace the chance to taste game meats like springbok, kudu, and oryx. Many restaurants and resorts serve game meat dishes, delivering a taste of Namibia's untamed delicacies.

Join a Traditional Meal: Consider sharing a traditional supper with a local family or at a community-run restaurant. This immersive tour will expose you to traditional foods and local warmth.

Taste Traditional Porridge: Don't miss the opportunity to enjoy oshifima, a traditional porridge prepared from mahangu (pearl millet) flour, generally served with meat or vegetable stew.

Indulge in Biltong: Sample biltong, Namibia's renowned dry and cured beef dish. It's an excellent on-the-go treat whether traveling or trekking.

Enjoy Local Beverages: Sip on local beverages like Namibian beer, such as Windhoek Lager, and experience traditional drinks like omagungu (fermented mahangu drink) and the sweet and sour juice of the marula fruit.

Participate in a Braai: A braai (barbecue) is a favorite Namibian social activity. Join a braai and enjoy grilled meats, salads, and side dishes in the company of locals.

Seek Out Regional Specialties: Each area in Namibia has its culinary peculiarities. While traveling to various regions, enquire about local delicacies peculiar to the region you're visiting.

Respect Local Customs: When dining like a native, respect local traditions and etiquette. For example, using your right hand to eat is conventional, and in rural regions, it's appropriate to greet and thank your hosts using traditional expressions.

Eating like a native in Namibia is an interesting experience that will link you with the country's cultural traditions and cuisine. Be brave, taste different meals, and connect with people to make the most of your gastronomic tour across this varied and lovely country.

Fun Facts:

Namibia is recognised for its bright and unpolluted night sky, making it a stargazer's delight. The country has been classified as an International Dark Sky Reserve, giving great astronomy opportunities.

ADVENTURE AND OUTDOOR ACTIVITIES

Safari and Wildlife Viewing

Namibia provides outstanding possibilities for safari and wildlife watching, making it a favorite vacation for nature enthusiasts and animal lovers. Here's everything you need to know about enjoying the finest of safari and wildlife watching in Namibia:

National Parks and Game Reserves: Namibia is home to various national parks and private game reserves, each providing distinct landscapes and rich species. Etosha National Park, Namib-Naukluft National Park, Bwabwata National Park, and NamibRand Nature Reserve are some of the main sites for safari adventures.

Game Drives: Game drives are the principal method to discover Namibia's wildlife-rich regions. Whether guided or self-driven, game drives take you to waterholes and vantage spots where you may observe a broad range of animals, including elephants, lions, giraffes, rhinos, zebras, and more.

Etosha Pan: Etosha National Park, with its wide Etosha Pan, is one of Africa's best wildlife watching sites.

The pan draws a myriad of species throughout the dry season, offering good possibilities for close encounters.

Desert-Adapted Wildlife: In Namibia's dry areas, such as Damaraland and the Namib Desert, you may watch desert-adapted animals such as desert elephants, desert lions, oryx, and springbok. Specialized tours and guides give insights into their distinctive adaptations.

Birdwatching: Namibia features a varied biodiversity, with over 700 bird species reported. Birdwatching lovers may view a variety of raptors, waterbirds, and desert-dwelling birds in varied environments.

Night Drives and Guided Walks: Some reserves and resorts provide night drives and guided walks, enabling you to see animal activity during the midnight hours and learn about the small critters and unique ecosystems.

Photography Opportunities: Namibia's beautiful scenery and rich animals give fantastic possibilities for wildlife photography. Capture amazing scenery, rare desert-adapted wildlife, and gorgeous sunsets throughout the wilderness.

Conservation Initiatives: Many resorts and reserves in Namibia are actively participating in animal conservation activities.

Supporting eco-friendly and community-based tourism can contribute to wildlife preservation and local communities.

Respect Wildlife and Environment: When on safari, conduct responsible wildlife watching and respect the natural environment. Adhere to park laws and standards, keep a safe distance from animals, and avoid feeding them.

Namibia's safari and wildlife watching excursions give an opportunity to interact with nature in its purest form. Whether you're visiting historic national parks, finding desert-adapted animals, or capturing compelling wildlife moments, a safari in Namibia guarantees unique experiences with the wild and the splendor of the African wilderness.

Dune Boarding and Desert Excursions

Dune boarding and desert tours are exhilarating and daring activities that enable you to see the grandeur and magnificence of Namibia's desert landscapes. Here's what you may anticipate while partaking in these activities:

Dune Boarding: Dune surfing, sometimes known as sandboarding, is a popular hobby in Namibia, notably in the Namib Desert between Swakopmund and Walvis Bay.

The sport includes sliding down sand dunes on a specially made board, akin to snowboarding but on sand. It gives an adrenaline-pumping experience and a unique way to engage with the desert landscape.

Desert Excursions: Desert excursions take you on guided trips across the breathtaking desert landscapes of Namibia. These trips may be in 4x4 cars, on quad bikes, or even on foot, depending on the region and the style of experience you desire.

Swakopmund and Walvis Bay: Swakopmund and Walvis Bay are famous starting sites for dune surfing and desert trips. Both areas provide spectacular coastline and desert views, making them perfect headquarters for exploring the nearby dunes.

Sossusvlei and Namib Desert: In the southern section of Namibia, you may go on desert trips to Sossusvlei and the Namib Desert. Here, you'll find some of the world's tallest sand dunes, including the renowned Dune 45, which is a favorite place for dawn photography.

Guided Tours: Desert tours are often supervised by trained guides who are informed about the desert environment, fauna, and safety procedures.

They will give you insights into the desert's distinctive flora and wildlife, as well as its geological aspects.

Quad Biking: If you want a more daring experience, quad riding across the desert is another exhilarating choice. You can cover more land and visit distant locations, enjoying the tranquility and magnificence of the desert.

Sunrise and Sunset Views: Both dune surfing and desert tours typically give the opportunity to watch stunning dawn and sunset views over the dunes. The fluctuating hues of the sand and the grandeur of the terrain produce memorable moments.

Safety Precautions: When partaking in these activities, it's crucial to follow safety recommendations issued by your tour operator or guide. This involves employing correct equipment and preserving the vulnerable desert environment.

Dune surfing and desert trips in Namibia provide a wonderful blend of excitement, awe-inspiring landscapes, and a connection with nature. Whether you're sliding down the dunes on a board or exploring the desert in a 4x4, these excursions will leave you with lasting memories of Namibia's spectacular vistas.

Hiking and Trekking

Namibia's various landscapes provide wonderful chances for hiking and trekking, enabling you to immerse yourself in the country's natural splendor and find hidden jewels. Here's what you may anticipate while partaking in hiking and trekking activities in Namibia:

Fish River Canyon Hiking Trail: The Fish River Canyon Hiking Trail is one of Namibia's most renowned and hard treks. It spans for around 90 kilometers (56 miles) along the Fish River Canyon, giving beautiful vistas and interactions with animals. It's a multi-day trek that demands high physical fitness and preparedness.

Naukluft Mountains: The Naukluft Mountains in the Namib-Naukluft National Park provide several hiking paths of differing durations and difficulty levels. These routes travel through spectacular vistas, mountain gorges, and lush river valleys, giving possibilities for birding and animal encounters.

Waterberg Plateau Park: Waterberg Plateau Park is recognised for its unusual sandstone plateau, which rises steeply from the surrounding lowlands. The park provides various hiking paths, including the Waterberg Plateau Trail, which rewards hikers with panoramic views from the plateau's peak.

Spitzkoppe: Spitzkoppe, often known as the Matterhorn of Namibia, is a stunning granite rock structure that draws climbers and hikers alike. There are many hiking routes surrounding Spitzkoppe, leading to old rock art and spectacular overlooks.

Brandberg Mountain: Brandberg Mountain is Namibia's tallest mountain, and it is known for its remarkable rock art dubbed "White Lady." Hiking to the peak of Brandberg is a tough but rewarding adventure, affording beautiful perspectives over the surrounding desert.

Desert Hikes: Some resorts and desert reserves provide guided desert treks, enabling you to experience the distinctive flora, wildlife, and geological aspects of Namibia's dry landscapes.

Etosha National Park: While largely renowned for wildlife drives, Etosha National Park also provides short hiking routes around some of its waterholes. These treks give you a chance to stretch your legs and view the park from a fresh perspective.

Remote and Guided Treks: For more daring hikers, there are distant and guided treks accessible in some places, allowing an opportunity to explore lesser-known areas and partake in more prolonged wilderness adventures.

When hiking and trekking in Namibia, it's necessary to be well-prepared, particularly considering weather conditions, water supplies, and physical fitness. It's best to join guided treks while exploring unknown terrains, as expert guides can boost your safety and understanding of the area's flora and animals. Whether you're seeking tough treks or leisurely walks, Namibia's hiking and trekking options give a meaningful connection with nature and an opportunity to observe the country's magnificent landscapes up close.

Water-based Activities

Namibia's water-based activities provide a refreshing contrast to its desert surroundings, enabling you to enjoy the country's coastline and river settings. Here are some great water-based activities to enjoy in Namibia:

Dolphin and Seal Cruises: In Walvis Bay and Swakopmund, you may embark on boat trips to observe lively dolphins and inquisitive seals in their natural environment. These trips sometimes feature possibilities for birding and lovely views of the coastline.

Kayaking: Kayaking is a popular pastime on Namibia's coastal waterways and rivers. Paddle along the Atlantic coast or explore the quiet waters of the Okavango River, immersing yourself in the spectacular landscape and animal sightings.

Birdwatching and Wetland Tours: Namibia is home to various wetlands and estuaries that attract a vast variety of bird species. Guided birding and wetland trips enable you to view many waterbirds, including flamingos, pelicans, and uncommon migratory species.

Fishing: For fishing aficionados, Namibia provides good options for both freshwater and saltwater fishing. The Zambezi and Kunene Rivers are known for angling, while coastal locations are good for beach and boat fishing.

Canoeing: Canoeing along the Zambezi and Okavango Rivers delivers a calm and immersive experience in Namibia's riverine landscapes. Guided canoe outings give an opportunity to watch animals and explore the rivers at a moderate pace.

Sunset Cruises: Sunset cruises are a tranquil way to appreciate the beauty of Namibia's coastline sunsets and riverbanks. Relax on board as the brilliant hues of the sunset sun reflect on the ocean.

Catamaran Tours: Catamaran trips provide a pleasant opportunity to explore Namibia's coastal waterways and enjoy the marine life.

These cruises sometimes include gourmet meals and beverages, delivering a wonderful experience on the open sea.

Houseboat Trips: Houseboat cruises on the Zambezi River and the Okavango Delta provide a unique combination of animal encounters and water-based leisure. Spend your days seeing animals from the luxury of your houseboat and enjoy starlit evenings on the water.

Namibia's water-based activities give a refreshing and wide selection of experiences, from seeing marine life and birding to exploring picturesque river vistas. Whether you like daring kayaking or peaceful boat tours, these activities provide a fascinating opportunity to interact with nature's aquatic treasures in Namibia.

Kayaking and Canoeing

Kayaking and canoeing in Namibia provide unique possibilities to explore the country's waterways, from tranquil rivers to the coastal seas of the Atlantic Ocean. Here's what you should anticipate while partaking in kayaking and canoeing sports in Namibia:

Kayaking on the Atlantic Coast: Kayaking along Namibia's Atlantic coastline, notably in the districts of Walvis Bay and Swakopmund, is a popular recreation. You may paddle over calm seas, seeing seals, dolphins, and numerous species that frequent the region.

Seal and Dolphin Encounters: Kayaking in Walvis Bay provides for up-close interactions with playful seals and inquisitive dolphins. These clever sea species regularly approach kayakers, providing for amazing encounters.

Birdwatching: As you kayak along the shore or in river estuaries, you'll have the chance to engage in birding. Namibia's coastal wetlands attract a variety of bird species, including flamingos, pelicans, and cormorants.

Kayaking in the Okavango River: The Okavango River, which forms part of Namibia's northern border, provides great canoeing and kayaking options. Paddle through rich riverine flora and watch varied species along the riverbanks.

Canoeing in the Zambezi Region: The Zambezi Region, historically known as the Caprivi Strip, is another wonderful site for canoeing and kayaking. Canoe along the Kwando and Zambezi Rivers, immersing yourself in the region's unique ecosystems.

Scenic Landscapes: Whether kayaking along the shore or canoeing on rivers, you'll be surrounded by breathtaking surroundings. From the dunes of the Atlantic coast to the rich greenery of riverbanks, the view is varied and appealing.

Guided Tours and Safety: Guided kayaking and canoeing trips are provided, conducted by qualified instructors who give safety briefings and share their expertise of the area's animals and ecosystem.

Sunset and Sunrise Paddles: Opt for sunset or dawn kayaking experiences to watch the shifting hues of the sky over the river. These calm encounters provide lovely moments in nature.

Suitable for All Skill Levels: Kayaking and canoeing in Namibia are suited for all ability levels, from beginners to expert paddlers. You may pick from numerous trip lengths and itineraries depending on your interests and skills.

Kayaking and canoeing in Namibia give a great opportunity to interact with nature and explore the country's water treasures. Whether you like coastal experiences with seals and dolphins or kayaking through the calm landscapes of rivers, these water-based activities guarantee remarkable interactions and spectacular vistas in the midst of Africa's untamed splendor.

Dolphin and Seal Cruises

Dolphin and seal excursions in Namibia provide a unique and intriguing experience, enabling you to interact with marine species in their natural environment. These cruises are especially popular in the coastal cities of Walvis Bay and Swakopmund. Here's what you can anticipate on a dolphin and seal tour in Namibia:

Marine Wildlife Encounters: During the tour, you'll get the chance to observe playful dolphins and inquisitive seals up close. Bottlenose and Heaviside's dolphins are regularly sighted, along with Cape fur seals that live the rocky coasts.

Boat Tours and Catamarans: Dolphin and seal tours are often done on robust boats or roomy catamarans, suited to give comfort and safety throughout the voyage.

Knowledgeable Guides: Experienced guides join the tours, delivering insightful commentary about marine life, coastal ecology, and the unique ecosystems found along Namibia's Atlantic coastline.

Birdwatching Opportunities: The tours also provide wonderful birding opportunities, as various seabirds, including pelicans, flamingos, cormorants, and terns, flourish in the coastal wetlands.

Educational and Interactive Experience: The guides regularly involve guests in engaging activities, such as feeding the seals or providing intriguing information about the behavior and ecology of the marine creatures.

Breathtaking Scenery: The cruises take you through the picturesque coastline, affording breathtaking views of the dunes, beaches, and the grandeur of the Atlantic Ocean.

Snacks & Refreshments: Many dolphin and seal tours serve light food and drinks on board, enabling you to relax and appreciate the view while tasting the coastal wind.

Sunrise and Sunset Cruises: Some operators provide dawn and sunset excursions, adding the magnificent experience of viewing the shifting hues of the sky over the sea.

Eco-friendly and Responsible Tourism: Most cruise companies in Namibia adhere to eco-friendly methods and responsible tourist rules, guaranteeing minimum effect on the marine creatures and their surroundings.

Dolphin and seal cruises in Namibia are family-friendly activities that appeal to guests of all ages. The opportunity to see dolphins happily swimming beside the boat and seals lounging on the shoreline produces memorable recollections of Namibia's wonderful marine life. Whether you're a wildlife enthusiast, a photography enthusiast, or just seeking a unique marine experience, a dolphin and seal tour is a great opportunity to interact with nature's marvels on the Atlantic coast.

Stargazing in Namibia's Dark Sky Reserves

Namibia's Dark Sky Reserves provide stargazing experiences like no other, delivering a stunning view of the night sky in its purest form. Here's what you may anticipate while stargazing in Namibia's Dark Sky Reserves:

Exceptional Night Sky Visibility: Namibia's Dark Sky Reserves, such as the NamibRand Nature Reserve and the Gamsberg Nature Reserve, are situated in distant places with low light pollution. This results in crystal-clear night sky and great viewing of stars, planets, and celestial events.

Milky Way with Constellations: In these pure black sky places, the Milky Way is seen in all its majesty, sweeping across the sky like a bright river. You can also readily see numerous constellations and star clusters that may be difficult to observe in urban surroundings.

Night Photography: The dark sky reserves provide wonderful chances for night photography. Capture amazing photographs of the Milky Way, star trails, and other cosmic phenomena using long exposure methods.

Guided Stargazing Tours: Many lodges and reserves in Namibia offer guided stargazing excursions conducted by qualified guides or local astronomers. These experts will point out stars, planets, and other celestial objects while giving unique insights about astronomy and the mythology behind constellations.

Meteor Showers and Celestial Events: If your visit coincides with a meteor shower or other celestial occurrences, such as eclipses or planetary conjunctions, you'll have an even more remarkable stargazing experience.

Peaceful and Tranquil Atmosphere: Stargazing in Namibia's Dark Sky Reserves delivers a feeling of peace and connection with the natural world. The lack of artificial light enables you to immerse yourself in the tranquil ambience of the night.

Astro Tourism and Astronomy Lodges: Some hotels in Namibia are devoted to astro tourism, featuring state-of-the-art observatories and stargazing platforms. These lodgings offer visitors with telescopes and other astronomy equipment for an improved stargazing experience.

Nighttime Wildlife Encounters: While stargazing, you may have the opportunity to watch nighttime wildlife activities, such as the sounds of faraway animals or the odd visit of inquisitive critters near the stargazing spot.

IMMERSING IN NAMIBIAN CULTURE

Indigenous People of Namibia

Namibia is home to a broad spectrum of indigenous peoples, each with its distinct customs, traditions, and languages. Here are some of the major indigenous groups in Namibia:

Ovambo: The Ovambo people are the biggest ethnic group in Namibia, inhabiting largely in the northern region of the country. They are noted for their diverse cultural traditions, including song, dance, and ceremonies.

Herero: The Herero people are mostly located in central and north-central Namibia. They have unique clothes, including the renowned Victorian-style costumes for ladies and military-style uniforms for men.

Himba: The Himba are a semi-nomadic ethnic group dwelling in the Kunene area of northeastern Namibia.

112

They are noted for their unusual look, traditional clothes, and intricate haircuts, frequently embellished with red ochre.

San (Bushmen): The San, commonly known as Bushmen, are one of the earliest indigenous communities in Namibia. They previously lived as hunter-gatherers in the Kalahari Desert and adjoining locations. Their comprehensive understanding of the environment and survival abilities are outstanding.

Nama: The Nama people mostly occupy southern Namibia. They have a strong cultural past and are noted for their unique Nama language, traditional music, and dances.

Damara: The Damara people are situated in central and western Namibia. They have a long history and have been noted for their abilities in metals, ceramics, and beading.

Himba: The Himba are a semi-nomadic ethnic group dwelling in the Kunene area of northeastern Namibia. They are noted for their unusual look, traditional clothes, and intricate haircuts, frequently embellished with red ochre.

These indigenous people have lived in peace with the land for millennia, and their rich cultural history continues to be a vital component of Namibia's character. The Namibian government respects the rights and cultural relevance of indigenous people and is dedicated to maintaining their traditions and way of life. Visitors visiting Namibia have the chance to connect with and learn from these communities, gaining a greater respect for their distinct cultures and contributions to the country's colorful tapestry.

San (Bushmen) Culture

The San, also known as Bushmen, are one of the oldest indigenous communities in Africa, having a rich cultural tradition that extends back thousands of years. They are originally hunter-gatherers and have occupied the areas of southern Africa, including Namibia, Botswana, South Africa, Angola, and Zimbabwe. Here are some significant features of San culture:

Hunter-Gatherer Lifestyle: Traditionally, the San people have been hunter-gatherers, depending on their intimate understanding of the natural environment to locate food and water. They employ a mix of hunting, trapping, and gathering to maintain their communities.

Language and Click Sounds: The San people have a unique language characterized by click consonants, which are peculiar sounds created by clicking the tongue on the roof of the mouth. diverse click sounds transmit diverse messages, making their language intriguing and sophisticated.

Art and Rock Paintings: The San are known for their rock art, which gives unique insights into their old way of life. These elaborate murals, unearthed in caves and rock shelters, portray scenes of hunting, dancing, and spiritual rites.

Spiritual Beliefs: San faith is profoundly entrenched in nature, and they have a great connection with the land and animals. They believe in the power of ancestor spirits and execute rituals to seek guidance and protection.

Gathering and Sharing Knowledge: Knowledge is handed down orally via storytelling and shared experiences. The San elders are regarded for their wisdom, and the society cherishes learning from their acquired knowledge.

Nomadic Lifestyle: In the past, the San people maintained a nomadic existence, migrating from one place to another in search of food and water. Today, some San groups have shifted to a more stable lifestyle, while others retain their semi-nomadic way of life.

Community and Kinship: San communities are close-knit, stressing collaboration and sharing within the community. Kinship relationships are crucial, and they depend on one other for mutual support.

Challenges & Preservation: Despite their rich cultural past, the San people have suffered several obstacles, including loss of land, marginalization, and prejudice. Efforts are being made to conserve and celebrate their culture via cultural centers, community initiatives, and advocacy.

The San people's way of life is profoundly connected with their environment, and their traditional traditions reflect a peaceful connection with nature. As industrialization and outside influences damage their traditional lifestyle, there is rising acknowledgment of the need to conserve and protect their distinct cultural identity and expertise. Visitors visiting San villages have the chance to obtain insights into their historical traditions, arts, and spiritual beliefs, contributing to the respect and preservation of this unique culture.

Himba Culture

The Himba people are an indigenous ethnic group dwelling in the Kunene area of northeastern Namibia. They have a distinct cultural identity and are noted for their unusual look, traditional attire, and rich rituals. Here are some significant features of Himba culture:

Traditional Dress and Appearance: The Himba are notable for their ornate traditional dress, which includes complex hairstyles, ornamented with a combination of red ochre, butterfat, and otjize (a blend of ochre and butterfat). This gives their hair a unique reddish tint and is considered a sign of beauty and cultural identity.

Use of Otjize: Otjize is a vital aspect of Himba culture. It is a combination of red ochre and butterfat that the Himba people put on their skin and hair. It not only protects them from the harsh desert temperature but also bears cultural importance, indicating their connection to the ground and the spiritual realm.

Semi-Nomadic Lifestyle: The Himba people historically practice a semi-nomadic lifestyle, traveling with their herds of cattle to locate grazing pastures and water supplies. They have a great awareness of their surroundings and depend on their animals for subsistence.

Herding and Livestock: Cattle play a significant part in Himba life, supplying people with food, clothes, and a source of money. The Himba are skillful herders, and livestock are a measure of a family's prestige and fortune.

Communal Living and Kinship: The Himba live in large family groupings, and communal living is a fundamental aspect of their culture. They lay a tremendous premium on familial relationships and collective decision-making.

Spiritual Beliefs and Ancestral Worship: Himba spirituality is strongly related to their surroundings and ancestors. They believe in a higher power and conduct ancestor worship, seeking guidance and protection from their ancestral spirits.

Gender Roles and Initiation Rituals: The Himba have different gender responsibilities, with males responsible for herding cattle and women taking care of the family and children. Young Himba boys and girls endure initiation rites as they journey into adulthood.

Oral Tradition and Storytelling: The Himba retain their history and cultural knowledge via oral traditions, including storytelling and songs that pass down their practises and values from one generation to the next.

Traditional Medicine: The Himba depend on traditional medicinal traditions to cure diseases and preserve good health. They employ medicinal herbs and traditional therapeutic practices handed down through centuries.

Himba culture is rich and profoundly based in their strong contact with the earth, animals, and their spiritual beliefs. Despite some contemporary influences, many Himba villages retain their ancient way of life, and attempts are being undertaken to conserve their distinct cultural legacy for future generations. Visitors visiting Himba villages have the chance to learn about their traditions, watch their way of life, and obtain a greater knowledge of their amazing culture.

Traditional Music and Dance

Traditional music and dance are vital components of Namibia's rich cultural history. Each of the country's indigenous ethnic groups has its distinct music and dance styles, representing its traditions, beliefs, and way of life. Here are some examples of traditional music and dance in Namibia:

Oviritje (Ovambo): Oviritje is a prominent traditional dance and music form among the Ovambo people. It combines rhythmic clapping, stomping, and body gestures, commonly done in a circle or line shape. The dance is accompanied by singing and the usage of traditional musical instruments like the ombalantu (lamellophone) and drums.

Otjihimba (Himba): The Himba people have their distinct form of music and dance called Otjihimba. Himba women generally lead the dance, exhibiting their lavish hairstyles and jewelry while swaying to the beat of traditional melodies.

Dance of the Makalani Palm (Damara): The Damara people have a dance inspired by the makalani palm tree. Dancers emulate the swinging of the palm fronds while wearing palm leaf skirts, producing a mesmerizing performance that shows their connection to nature.

Dancing on Stilts (Herero): The Herero people have a peculiar dance done on stilts called "Karakul," signifying the grace and beauty of the heron bird. Dancers wearing long, flowing skirts execute elaborate maneuvers on stilts, producing a visually spectacular spectacle.

Traditional San Music and Dance: The San people have distinct musical traditions, involving chanting, clapping, and rhythmic dances. San dances generally mirror animal motions and have spiritual importance in their traditional rites.

Marimba and Drumming (Various Ethnic Groups): Marimba music and drumming are common among numerous ethnic groups in Namibia. Marimbas, xylophone-like instruments, are performed in groups, generating colorful tunes. Drumming is a vital feature of traditional festivals and rituals.

Traditional Wedding Dances: Various ethnic groups in Namibia have unique wedding dances, which are passionate and exuberant celebrations of love and togetherness. These dances sometimes entail the whole town coming together to commemorate the newlyweds.

Storytelling via Dance: Many traditional dances in Namibia contain a narrative component, relaying historical events, mythology, or moral teachings via movement and gestures.

Traditional music and dance play a major part in maintaining and celebrating Namibia's unique cultural history. These art forms continue to be a significant element of community meetings, festivals, and cultural events, keeping historical customs and traditions alive for years to come. Visitors visiting Namibia have the chance to see these bright and engaging performances and develop a greater understanding for the country's rich cultural variety.

Craft Markets and Souvenir Shopping

Craft markets and souvenir shopping are enjoyable experiences in Namibia, providing tourists the opportunity to explore the country's thriving arts and crafts sector and take home unique memories. Here's what you can anticipate while shopping for souvenirs in Namibia:

Craft Markets and Curio Shops: Throughout Namibia, you'll discover artisan markets and curio stores, particularly in important tourist sites like Windhoek, Swakopmund, and Opuwo. These marketplaces provide a broad choice of handcrafted items and traditional souvenirs.

Handmade Crafts: Namibia's craft markets offer a range of handcrafted products manufactured by local craftsmen. You'll discover wonderfully carved wooden sculptures, beaded jewelry, woven baskets, traditional ceramics, and leather products.

Himba and Herero Crafts: Some artisan fairs specialize in selling goods manufactured by the Himba and Herero cultures. You may discover unusual things like Himba jewelry made of copper and shells or Herero garments, embellished with bright designs and needlework.

San Art and Crafts: San art, including paintings and craftwork, is also offered at some markets. These works frequently represent images from traditional San life, fauna, and environment.

Namibian Gemstones and Minerals: Namibia is noted for its enormous resources of gemstones and minerals. You may discover wonderfully created jewelry containing gemstones like tourmaline, amethyst, and topaz.

Recycled and Sustainable Crafts: Some craftsmen produce items utilizing recycled materials, encouraging sustainability and environmental conscience. Look for goods created from recycled glass, cans, and scrap metal.

Bargaining and Fair Trade: Bargaining is a typical activity at artisan fairs in Namibia. However, try to be courteous and fair in your discussions. Additionally, several marketplaces encourage fair trade policies, ensuring that craftsmen get fair recompense for their labor.

Cultural Interaction: Shopping at craft fairs gives a chance to meet with local craftsmen and learn about their craft processes and cultural value of their goods.

Unique and Meaningful Souvenirs: Souvenir shopping in Namibia enables you to locate one-of-a-kind artifacts that reflect the spirit of the country's culture and surroundings, making them significant memories of your adventure.

When buying souvenirs in Namibia, consider supporting local craftsmen and community programmes that encourage sustainable tourism and the preservation of indigenous crafts. Souvenir buying not only enables you to take home a piece of Namibia but also supports the lives of the brilliant artists who continue to carry down their craft traditions from generation to generation.

SUSTAINABILITY AND RESPONSIBLE TRAVEL

Ethical Wildlife Encounters

Ethical wildlife interactions are vital to guarantee the well-being of animals and the protection of their natural habitats. When participating in animal adventures in Namibia or any other place, consider the following criteria for ethical encounters:

Choose Responsible Tour Operators: Select tour providers and guides that value the welfare of animals and adhere to ethical methods. Look for firms who are devoted to conservation and reduce their influence on the environment.

Avoid Wildlife Interaction: Avoid wildlife interactions that entail direct connection with wild animals, particularly those that may be used for entertainment reasons. Resist activities like elephant riding or close contact with caged predators.

Observe from a Distance: Opt for activities that enable you to watch animals from a safe and respectful distance. This guarantees that animals are neither distracted or worried by human presence.

Respect Wildlife Behavior: Observe and appreciate the natural behavior of animals. Avoid actions that may excite or upset them, such as making loud sounds or approaching too near.

Support Conservation Efforts: Choose animal interactions that help to conservation efforts and benefit local communities. Your visit should help safeguard animals and their habitats and give advantages to the local economy.

Follow Park Rules and Guidelines: When visiting national parks or protected areas, adhere to the restrictions and standards imposed by park officials. These restrictions are aimed to conserve species and their habitats.

No Feeding or Touching Wildlife: Do not feed wild animals, since it might disturb their normal diet and behavior. Additionally, avoid handling animals, since this might spread illnesses and disturb them.

Respect Wildlife Habitats: Stay on approved paths and roads to limit your influence on animal habitats. Avoid off-road driving and respect prohibited areas.

Educate Yourself: Educate yourself on the animals you meet, their behavior, and their significance in the ecosystem. Learning about animals creates a greater respect and knowledge of their value.

Report Illegal Activities: If you notice any unlawful activity relating to wildlife, such as poaching of wildlife trafficking, report it to the proper authorities or groups working to prevent such practices.

By emphasizing ethical wildlife interactions, you contribute to the conservation of Namibia's extraordinary biodiversity and help secure a sustainable future for its wildlife and natural heritage. Responsible tourist practices promote conservation efforts and enable local populations to cohabit happily with the distinct and varied fauna of the country.

Supporting Local Communities

Supporting local communities is a vital aspect of ethical and sustainable tourism in Namibia. Here are some ways you may have a good influence and contribute to the well-being of local communities during your visit:

Choose Community-Based Tourism: Opt for community-based tourism activities that directly benefit local people. Look for lodgings, excursions, and activities that are owned and run by residents of the community.

Buy Local Products: Purchase souvenirs, crafts, and items from local craftsmen and merchants at markets. Buying directly from people helps sustain their livelihoods and supports traditional crafts and cultural heritage.

Dine at Local Restaurants: Eat at locally-owned eateries and enjoy traditional Namibian delicacies. This helps the local economy and enables you to enjoy the country's rich culinary traditions.

Engage with the Community: Interact with local people politely and learn about their way of life, traditions, and customs. Engaging in cultural exchange increases mutual understanding and respect.

Volunteer with Responsible Organizations: If you prefer to give back to the community, try volunteering with respected groups that concentrate on social and environmental issues. Ensure that your talents and efforts coincide with the needs and objectives of the community.

Respect Local Customs: Familiarize oneself with local customs and traditions and show respect for cultural standards. This involves dressing modestly while visiting traditional villages and obtaining permission before taking images.

Conserve Resources: Be aware of water and energy consumption, particularly in locations with limited resources. Follow eco-friendly habits to limit your environmental effect and contribute to sustainable living.

Hire Local Guides: When scheduling excursions or safaris, hire local guides who have in-depth knowledge of the region and animals. Hiring local guides helps their livelihoods and guarantees a more genuine experience.

Donate to Local Projects: If you are enthusiastic about supporting particular community projects or environmental activities, consider making contributions to local groups working towards good change.

Be Mindful of Wildlife: Observe animals properly and follow instructions to conserve their natural habitats. Responsible wildlife interactions assist in the conservation of Namibia's unique species.

By supporting local communities, you may help to the preservation of Namibia's cultural heritage, stimulate sustainable development, and build a friendly interaction between visitors and local inhabitants. Responsible tourism practices give chances for empowerment and economic progress while ensuring that the country's natural and cultural riches be appreciated for generations to come.

Reducing Environmental Impact

Reducing your environmental effect when visiting Namibia is vital for conserving its spectacular natural landscapes and unique ecosystems. Here are some suggestions to help decrease your impact and encourage sustainable tourism:

Choose Sustainable Accommodations: Stay at eco-friendly hotels or lodgings that promote energy efficiency, water conservation, and waste reduction. Some hotels in Namibia are designed using sustainable materials and powered by renewable energy sources.

Practice Responsible Waste Management: Dispose of garbage appropriately and participate in recycling initiatives wherever possible. Avoid single-use plastics and carry reusable water bottles and bags.

Conserve Water: Namibia is a semi-arid country, therefore water conservation is crucial. Take brief showers and use water wisely. Report any water leaks to the lodge or accommodation staff.

Energy Efficiency: Turn off lights, air conditioning, and other electrical equipment while not in use. Unplug chargers and devices to reduce phantom energy use.

Use Sustainable Transportation: Consider taking public transit or sharing rides while going inside cities. For longer trips, choose for eco-friendly transit choices like buses or trains.

Choose Responsible Tour Operators: Select tour providers who stress eco-friendly operations and animal protection. Look for those with credentials or links with sustainable tourism groups.

Respect Wildlife and their Habitats: Observe animals from a distance and respect park regulations and standards. Do not disturb or feed animals, and avoid harming coral reefs or other vulnerable habitats.

Support Conservation Initiatives: Contribute to animal conservation efforts by visiting reputable wildlife sanctuaries and giving to recognised conservation groups operating in Namibia.

Minimize Plastic Use: Carry a reusable water bottle, shopping bag, and utensils to avoid using single-use plastics on your trip.

Learn & Educate: Educate yourself on Namibia's environmental issues and the necessity of conservation. Share this information with other tourists and motivate them to be ecologically conscientious.

By adopting these eco-friendly activities, you can help safeguard Namibia's natural beauty and biodiversity for future generations. Responsible tourism and conscious travel choices play a critical part in ensuring that Namibia's spectacular landscapes, wildlife, and cultural legacy continue to flourish in harmony with sustainable development.

PERFECT ITINERARIES FOR DIFFERENT KINDS OF TRAVELERS

Wildlife Enthusiast's Safari Adventure

Day 1: Arrival in Windhoek
- Arrive at Windhoek, Namibia's capital city.
- Rest and acclimatize to the local time.
- Explore the city's sights and taste local food.

Day 2: Drive to Etosha National Park
- Depart for Etosha National Park, a famous wildlife site.
- Check-in at your lodging or tent within the park.
- Afternoon game drive to observe elephants, lions, giraffes, and more.

Day 3: Full Day Game Drives in Etosha
- Embark on full-day game drives to experience the park's different ecosystems.
- Visit water holes filled with animals and witness predators in action.
- Enjoy a picnic meal in nature.

Day 4: Etosha to Damaraland
- Depart Etosha and proceed to Damaraland, noted for its distinctive scenery.

- En route, view the ancient rock engravings at Twyfelfontein.
- Check-in at your lodge and relax in the picturesque surroundings.

Day 5: Desert-Adapted Wildlife in Damaraland
- Explore Damaraland's desert-adapted fauna, including desert elephants and rhinos.
- Learn about the conservation efforts to safeguard these magnificent animals.

Day 6: Swakopmund
- Drive to Swakopmund, a beach town with a combination of German architecture and Namibian charm.
- Enjoy a relaxed day with optional activities like sand boarding or quad biking.

Day 7: Boat Cruise in Walvis Bay
- Take a boat trip in Walvis Bay to observe marine animals, including seals, dolphins, and seagulls.
- Enjoy fresh oysters and refreshments on board.

Day 8: Skeleton Coast National Park
- Embark on a picturesque flight or drive to Skeleton Coast National Park.
- Explore the barren but intriguing vistas, shipwrecks, and distinctive dunes.

Day 9: Sossusvlei and Namib Desert

- Depart for Sossusvlei, home of the renowned red sand dunes of the Namib Desert.
- Climb the dunes and observe the dawn over the wide desert landscape.

Day 10: Balloon Safari and Departure

- Optional hot air balloon tour above the Namib Desert at dawn.
- Depart for Windhoek for your further adventure or flight back home.

This wildlife enthusiast's safari adventure itinerary delivers an unparalleled experience of Namibia's various landscapes and magnificent animals. From the huge plains of Etosha to the desert-adapted species of Damaraland and the spectacular dunes of Sossusvlei, this safari tour offers amazing experiences with Namibia's outstanding natural riches.

Cultural Immersion and Community Experience

Day 1: Arrival in Windhoek

- Arrive at Windhoek, Namibia's capital city.
- Check-in at a locally-owned guesthouse or eco-lodge to support the community.

- Take a city tour to learn about Namibia's history and culture.

Day 2: Visit a Himba Village
- Travel to a Himba community in the Kunene area.
- Experience an actual cultural encounter with the Himba people.
- Learn about their traditional lifestyle, rituals, and crafts.

Day 3: Community Projects in Damaraland
- Visit community initiatives in Damaraland that concentrate on sustainable development.
- Participate in activities like gardening, crafts, or educational programs.
- Interact with local community members and learn about their efforts.

Day 4: Traditional Dance and Music Workshop
- Attend a traditional dance and music workshop in a local village.
- Learn traditional songs, dances, and musical instruments.
- Engage in cultural performances with community people.

Day 5: San (Bushmen) Cultural Experience

- Head to a San settlement in the Kalahari Desert.
- Join the San tribe in hunting and gathering activities.
- Listen to ancient legends and learn about their strong relationship with nature.

Day 6: Volunteer at a Wildlife Sanctuary

- Volunteer in a wildlife sanctuary working on conservation projects.
- Assist with animal care, environmental research, or educational activities.
- Contribute to the rehabilitation and preservation of Namibia's wildlife.

Day 7: Community Crafts and Souvenir Shopping

- Visit craft fairs in local towns to support craftspeople.
- Purchase homemade items and souvenirs directly from local merchants.
- Engage with craftsmen and learn about their craft traditions.

Day 8: Traditional Cooking Experience

- Participate in a traditional culinary experience with a local family.
- Learn to create Namibian delicacies and share a group lunch.

- Immerse yourself in the tastes and culinary traditions of Namibia.

Day 9: Explore Swakopmund's Cultural Heritage
- Explore Swakopmund's combination of German and Namibian culture.
- Visit local art galleries, museums, and artisan stores.
- Interact with people and learn about their cultural heritage

Day 10: Departure from Windhoek
- Return to Windhoek for your departure.
- Reflect on your cultural immersion experiences and wave goodbye to Namibia.

This cultural immersion and community experience programme gives a meaningful trip into the heart of Namibia's different cultures. Through engaging with local communities, participating in cultural events, and supporting community projects, you will get a greater knowledge of Namibia's rich cultural history and contribute to sustainable and responsible tourism practices.

Desert and Dune Exploration

Day 1: Arrival in Windhoek

- Arrive at Windhoek, Namibia's capital city.
- Check-in at your hotel and recuperate after your trip.
- Explore the city's attractions, including the Christuskirche and Independence Memorial Museum.

Day 2: Namib Desert - Sesriem

- Depart for Sesriem, the entrance to the Namib Desert.
- Explore the beautiful dunes at Elim Dune or Dune 45 for sunset views.
- Stay overnight at a lodge or camping near Sesriem.

Day 3: Sossusvlei and Deadvlei

- Early early trip to Sossusvlei to see the sunrise over the dunes.
- Hike atop Big Daddy or Big Mama dune for panoramic sights.
- Visit Deadvlei, a strange clay pit surrounded by old, dead camel thorn trees.
- Return to your hotel in Sesriem for the night.

Day 4: Sesriem Canyon and Naukluft Mountains

- Explore the spectacular Sesriem Canyon, a small ravine created by the Tsauchab River.
- Drive to the Naukluft Mountains, where you may go on picturesque walks and observe rare flora and wildlife.
- Spend the night in a lodge or campground in the Naukluft region.

Day 5: Swakopmund

- Drive to Swakopmund, a lovely seaside hamlet located between the desert and the Atlantic Ocean.
- Enjoy a relaxing day visiting the town's colonial buildings and beach promenade.
- Consider extra activities like quad biking or a beautiful flight over the dunes.

Day 6: Sandwich Harbour Excursion

- Take a guided 4x4 adventure to Sandwich Harbour, a rare coastal wetland surrounded by towering dunes.
- Spot a variety of birds and possibly even animals at the water's edge.
- Return to Swakopmund for another night.

Day 7: Moon Landscape and Welwitschia Plains

- Drive to the Moon scene, a bizarre desert scene mimicking the lunar surface.
- Visit the Welwitschia Plains, where you may observe ancient Welwitschia mirabilis plants, some over 1,000 years old.
- Return to Swakopmund for your final night by the sea.

Day 8: Return to Windhoek

- Depart from Swakopmund and drive back to Windhoek.
- Visit the Namibian Craft Centre for last-minute souvenir purchasing.
- Spend your last evening in Windhoek and reflect about your desert and dune tour.

Day 9: Departure from Windhoek

- Transfer to the airport for your departure from Namibia.
- Leave with amazing recollections of your desert journey in this beautiful country.

Family-friendly Namibian Adventure

Day 1: Arrival in Windhoek

- Arrive at Windhoek, Namibia's capital city.

- Check-in at a family-friendly hotel or lodge and unwind after your adventure.
- Explore the city's attractions, such as the Zoo Park or the Avis Dam Nature Reserve.

Day 2: Cheetah Conservation Fund
- Depart for the Cheetah Conservation Fund in Otjiwarongo.
- Learn about cheetah conservation initiatives and the necessity of conserving these majestic animals.
- Enjoy a family-friendly tour and witness cheetahs up close.

Day 3: Okonjima Nature Reserve
- Visit the Okonjima Nature Reserve, home of the AfriCat Foundation.
- Join guided activities best for families, such as nature hikes or tracking leopard and hyena.
- Stay overnight in family-friendly lodging inside the reserve.

Day 4: Waterberg Plateau Park
- Drive to the Waterberg Plateau Park.
- Explore the park on a guided family-friendly trek, observing animals and enjoying gorgeous vistas.

- Have a picnic lunch and potentially sight rare wildlife like the roan antelope.

Day 5: Namib Desert - Namib-Naukluft National Park

- Depart for the Namib Desert and the Namib-Naukluft National Park.
- Check-in at a family-friendly lodge near Sesriem or Sossusvlei.
- Enjoy a peaceful evening beneath the beautiful desert sky.

Day 6: Dune Adventure

- Embark on a fun-filled family dune experience.
- Climb the dunes, ride down the hills, and capture great shots amid the gorgeous desert scenery.
- Explore Deadvlei with its weird, petrified trees.

Day 7: Swakopmund

- Drive to Swakopmund, a beach town with a range of family activities.
- Enjoy a peaceful day on the beach or try sandboarding on the dunes.
- Take a family-friendly boat tour in Walvis Bay to observe seals and dolphins.

Day 8: Living Desert Tour

- Join a Living Desert Tour to learn about the unique desert-adapted species.
- Your guide will show out sidewinders, desert chameleons, and other wonderful desert dwellers.
- Spend another night in Swakopmund.

Day 9: Return to Windhoek

- Drive back to Windhoek, with an optional stop at the Spitzkoppe for a family trek.
- Explore the Namibian Craft Centre for unique gifts.
- Spend your final evening in Windhoek, reflecting on your family-friendly Namibian journey.

Day 10: Departure from Windhoek

- Transfer to the airport for your departure from Namibia.
- Leave with fond recollections of your wonderful family experience in this beautiful country.

Self-Drive Expedition across Namibia

Day 1: Arrival in Windhoek

- Arrive at Windhoek, Namibia's capital city.
- Pick up your rental vehicle and check-in to a hotel or guesthouse.
- Explore the city's attractions, including the Alte Feste Museum and the artisan markets.

Day 2: Kalahari Desert - Intu Afrika Kalahari Game Reserve

- Depart for the Kalahari Desert.
- Drive to the Intu Afrika Kalahari wildlife Reserve and enjoy a guided wildlife drive.
- Experience the expanse of the Kalahari and observe rare desert species.

Day 3: Fish River Canyon

- Drive to the Fish River Canyon, one of the biggest canyons in the world.
- Take in the spectacular views from the canyon's rim.
- Enjoy a relaxing day exploring the local region.

Day 4: Lüderitz

- Drive to the beach town of Lüderitz.
- Explore the ghost town of Kolmanskop, a former diamond mining village.
- Visit the renowned Felsenkirche and see the colonial architecture.

Day 5: Namib Desert - Namib-Naukluft National Park

- Head to the Namib Desert and the Namib-Naukluft National Park.

- Check-in at a lodge or campground near Sesriem or Sossusvlei.
- Relax and ready for your desert excursions.

Day 6: Sossusvlei and Deadvlei

- Early early trip to Sossusvlei for dawn across the dunes.
- Hike atop Dune 45 or Big Daddy for amazing views.
- Visit Deadvlei and its spooky, dried-up trees.

Day 7: Swakopmund

- Drive to Swakopmund, a beach town with a blend of German and Namibian culture.
- Enjoy a relaxing day exploring the town or attempting adrenaline-fueled sports like sand boarding or skydiving.

Day 8: Skeleton Coast National Park

- Embark on a picturesque trip to Skeleton Coast National Park.
- Explore the dismal but intriguing scenery and shipwrecks along the shore.
- Overnight in a lodge or campground within the park.

Day 9: Damaraland

- Drive to Damaraland, noted for its harsh terrain and desert-adapted animals.
- Visit the prehistoric rock carvings at Twyfelfontein, a UNESCO World Heritage Site.
- Look out for desert-adapted elephants and other animals.

Day 10: Etosha National Park

- Head to Etosha National Park, one of Africa's best wildlife parks.
- Enter the park via the Anderson Gate and start your self-guided game drives.
- Spend the night at a campground or lodge within the park.

Day 11-12: Exploring Etosha

- Spend two full days exploring Etosha's various landscapes and rich wildlife.
- Visit numerous waterholes, where animals congregate to drink, and see predators and their victims.

Day 13: Return to Windhoek

- Drive back to Windhoek.
- Return your rental vehicle and check-in at your hotel.
- Enjoy a goodbye supper and reflect on your self-drive journey throughout Namibia.

Day 14: Departure from Windhoek
- Transfer to the airport for your departure from Namibia.
- Leave with wonderful recollections of your self-drive vacation in this beautiful country.

Relaxation and Coastal Getaway in Swakopmund

Day 1: Arrival in Swakopmund
- Arrive at Swakopmund, a picturesque beach town in Namibia.
- Check-in at a beachfront hotel or a guesthouse with ocean views.
- Relax and relax after your travel by walking along the beach or enjoying the seaside air.

Day 2: Dolphin and Seal Cruise
- Embark on a morning dolphin and seal cruise in Walvis Bay.
- Spot playful dolphins, inquisitive seals, and numerous seabirds in their natural environment.
- Enjoy fresh oysters and refreshments aboard while taking in the picturesque splendor of the coastline.

Day 3: Desert Adventure - Sandwich Harbour

- Experience the best of both worlds with a desert journey to Sandwich Harbour.
- Join a guided 4x4 adventure to discover the towering dunes and the coastal marshes.
- Enjoy amazing views at the meeting point between the desert and the ocean.

Day 4: Quad Biking and Dune Boarding
- Spend the morning quad riding in the dunes near Swakopmund.
- Try your hand at dune boarding, a thrilling pastime where you slide down the dunes on a board.
- Afterward, indulge yourself to a peaceful spa treatment or spend a quiet day at the beach.

Day 5: Living Desert Tour
- Embark on a Living Desert Tour to experience the interesting wildlife of the Namib Desert.
- Your skilled guide will expose you to sidewinders, geckos, and other desert dwellers.
- Enjoy the chance to shoot these unusual animals in their natural setting.

Day 6: Swakopmund Museum and Art Galleries
- Take a cultural tour to Swakopmund's museum and art galleries.

- Learn about Namibia's history, marine life, and the local cultural scene.
- Enjoy a lovely meal at one of the town's numerous cafés or eateries.

Day 7: Beach Leisure Day
- Spend a quiet day at the beach, lounging under the sun.
- Engage in beach activities like beach volleyball or constructing sandcastles.
- Enjoy a beachside supper with ocean views.

Day 8: Return to Windhoek
- Depart from Swakopmund and drive back to Windhoek.
- Reflect on your pleasant beach break and appreciate the memories of your stay in Swakopmund.

Day 9: Departure from Windhoek
- Transfer to the airport for your departure from Namibia.
- Leave with a feeling of peace and refreshment after your pleasant beach retreat in Swakopmund.

Photography and Stargazing Expedition

Day 1: Arrival in Windhoek

- Arrive at Windhoek, Namibia's capital city.
- Check-in at your accommodation and recuperate after your adventure.
- Familiarize yourself with your camera gear and prepare for your photographic adventure.

Day 2: Drive to Sossusvlei
- Depart for Sossusvlei in the Namib Desert.
- Capture the magnificent vistas and renowned dunes at sunset.
- Set up for stargazing in the desert.

Day 3: Sunrise Photography in Deadvlei
- Rise early for a dawn photography session at Deadvlei.
- Capture the bizarre environment with the contrast of red dunes and white clay pan.
- Explore other adjacent dunes for further picture options.

Day 4: Sesriem Canyon and Naukluft Mountains
- Visit the Sesriem Canyon for unusual photographs of the tight gorge.
- Drive to the Naukluft Mountains and capture the magnificent scenery and fauna.
- Capture the stars and Milky Way at night.

Day 5: Drive to Swakopmund

- Travel to Swakopmund, a beach village with numerous shooting options.
- Photograph colonial buildings, dunes meeting the sea, and the shoreline.
- Enjoy stars on the beach at night.

Day 6: Coastal Photography
- Spend the day shooting the gorgeous coastline and marine life.
- Take a boat cruise in Walvis Bay to catch seagulls, seals, and dolphins.
- Stargaze on the beach again, taking advantage of the beautiful coastal sky.

Day 7: Sandwich Harbour Excursion
- Join a guided photography excursion to Sandwich Harbour.
- Capture the stunning sceneries where desert dunes meet the Atlantic Ocean.
- Enjoy the chance to shoot animals in the region.

Day 8: Drive to Spitzkoppe
- Travel to Spitzkoppe, renowned as the "Matterhorn of Namibia."
- Photograph the old granite peaks around sunset and stargazing at night.
- Set up your camera for long exposure photographs of the starry night sky.

Day 9: Spitzkoppe Photography

- Spend the day shooting the rock formations and the surrounding scenery.
- Capture the Milky Way rising over the Spitzkoppe for beautiful astrophotography.
- Reflect on your photographic adventure in this beautiful location.

Day 10: Return to Windhoek

- Drive back to Windhoek, soaking in the beauty along the way.
- Use this last day to analyze your photographic catches and make any final photos.
- Prepare your equipment for the drive back home.

Day 11: Departure from Windhoek

- Transfer to the airport for your departure from Namibia.
- Leave with a portfolio of magnificent photographs from your photography and stargazing adventure in this enchanting country.

Fun Facts:

The unique combination of cultures in Namibia enables tourists to enjoy a complex tapestry of traditions, from the Himba and San people to the different cuisines and customs of the country.

PRACTICAL TIPS FOR AMERICAN AND EUROPEAN TRAVELERS AND TOURISTS

Basic Phrases in English and Local Languages

The official language of Namibia is English. It is frequently used for communication, notably in government, education, and commercial sectors. English serves as a uniting language in this linguistically heterogeneous country.

Apart from English, there are other local languages spoken by distinct ethnic groups. Some of the important local languages of Namibia include:

☐ Oshiwambo (spoken by the Ovambo people)

☐ Otjiherero (spoken by the Herero people)

☐ Damara/Nama (spoken by the Damara and Nama people)

☐ Afrikaans (derived from Dutch and extensively used owing to Namibia's colonial past)

☐ German (also spoken by certain Namibians owing to the country's historical links with Germany)

These native languages are a vital component of Namibia's cultural legacy and are still actively utilized in daily communication within their individual communities. While English is generally understood, learning a few words in the local languages may improve your travel experience and encourage better contacts with the local people.

Here are some simple phrases in English and local languages often used in Namibia:

Oshiwambo (spoken by the Ovambo people):
- Hello - Ondjala / Mwa-le-le
- Good morning - Wa-mu-li po?
- Thank you - O-mu-nan-ge
- Yes - Ee / Yee No - Ahee

Herero (spoken by the Herero people):
- Hello - Wa-ru na
- Good morning - Oho-mu-ni-ve po?
- Thank you - O-mu-he-rero
- Yes - Ee / Yee No - Ahee

Damara/Nama (spoken by the Damara and Nama people):

- Hello - Gei / Na-gei
- Good morning - Oho-mu-tje po?

- Thank you - A-ai / Gai-aeb
- Yes - Ee / Yee No - Ahee

Afrikaans (often spoken in Namibia):
- Hello - Hallo
- Good morning - Goeie môre
- Thank you - Dankie
- Yes - Ja No - Nee

German (owing to Namibia's colonial past, German is also spoken by certain locals):
- Hello - Hallo
- Good morning - Guten Morgen
- Thank you - Danke
- Yes - Ja
- No - Nein

Namibia is a linguistically varied country, and although English is commonly spoken, learning a few words in the local languages may improve your cultural experience and help you interact with the local populations during your stay.

Currency and Banking

The currency used in Namibia is the Namibian Dollar (NAD), indicated by the sign "$" or "N$" to differentiate it from other dollar currencies.

The money is divisible into 100 cents, and coins are available in quantities of 5, 10, 50 cents, and 1, 5 Namibian dollars. Banknotes are issued in denominations of 10, 20, 50, 100, and 200 Namibian dollars.

In addition to the Namibian Dollar, the South African Rand (ZAR) is also recognised as legal money across Namibia. The Namibian Dollar is tied to the South African Rand at a 1:1 exchange rate, therefore both currencies are used interchangeably in everyday transactions. When making purchases or withdrawing money from ATMs, you may get change in either Namibian Dollars or South African Rands.

Money Matters:

ATMs: ATMs are extensively accessible in major cities and towns in Namibia, and most accept major international credit and debit cards. Visa and Mastercard are usually accepted. However, it is advised to carry some cash for rural places where ATMs may be limited.

Credit Cards: Credit cards are generally accepted at hotels, lodges, restaurants, and major stores in metropolitan areas. However, in more rural and distant places, cash is frequently the favored mode of payment.

Money Exchange: You may exchange foreign money at banks, exchange offices, and certain hotels in big cities like Windhoek and Swakopmund. US Dollars, Euros, and South African Rands are the most widely accepted international currencies for exchange.

Safety: As with any trip, it's vital to be careful with your money and possessions. Keep your cash, credit cards, and critical papers protected, and avoid exhibiting big quantities of money in public.

Overall, Namibia is a pretty secure and traveler-friendly country when it comes to money concerns. However, it's always a good idea to be aware of the local currency, payment choices, and any costs before your trip to guarantee a seamless and happy experience.

Recommended Packing List

When going to Namibia as an American or European, it's necessary to pack properly to guarantee a comfortable and pleasurable journey. Here's a suggested packing list:

Clothing:
- Lightweight, breathable apparel for hot days.
- Long-sleeved shirts and leggings for sun protection.

- A light jacket or sweater for cold nights, particularly in arid locations.
- suitable footwear for outdoor activities such as hiking boots or walking shoes.
- Sandals or flip-flops for beach and pleasure.

Sun Protection:
- Sunscreen with high SPF.
- A hat or cap with a wide brim to block the sun.
- Sunglasses with UV protection.

Personal Essentials:
- Passport and essential travel papers.
- Prescription pills and a small first aid kit.
- Insect repellant for protection against mosquitoes.
- Personal toiletries and hygiene goods.

Photography Equipment:
- Camera includes extra batteries and memory cards.
- Binoculars for wildlife and bird viewing.

Travel Adapters and Chargers:
- Power adapters suited for Namibia's electrical outlets (Type D and Type M plugs).
- Chargers for electrical gadgets (phones, cameras, etc.).

Travel Insurance:
- Comprehensive travel insurance covers medical emergencies and trip disruptions.

Money and Wallet Essentials:
- Cash in Namibian Dollars or South African Rands for distant places without ATMs.
- Credit/debit cards for bigger cities and villages.

Daypack: A small daypack for excursions and day trips.

Water Bottle: A reusable water container to remain hydrated, particularly in the desert.

Lightweight Rain Jacket: A packable rain jacket or poncho for unexpected rain showers.

Binoculars: Binoculars for wildlife and bird viewing.

Travel papers: Copies of vital travel papers (passport, visa, insurance) in case of loss.

Adventure Gear (if applicable): If you want to indulge in sports like dune boarding or quad riding, suitable clothes and closed-toe shoes are suggested.

Remember that Namibia may have varied temperatures and weather conditions, so it's vital to prepare for both hot days and chilly nights. Additionally, packing light is important, since it allows for simple movement throughout your journey.

Keep in mind that the packing list may change based on the precise activities you want to perform and the time of year you visit. It's usually a good idea to check the weather prediction and modify your packing list appropriately.

Electrical Outlets and Voltage

In Namibia, the electrical outlets used are of two types: Type D and Type M.

Type D outlets feature three circular pins and are popularly known as the "Old British" or "Indian" plugs. Type M outlets feature three huge, spherical pins and are referred to as the "South African" plugs. Both varieties are employed in various regions around the country.

The standard voltage in Namibia is 220-240 volts, and the standard frequency is 50 hertz. If you are going from a country with a different voltage or plug type, you will need a travel adapter to operate your electrical equipment in Namibia.

When preparing for your vacation, be sure to carry the necessary travel adapter or converter to match the Type D or Type M outlets. This will enable you to charge your gadgets and operate electrical appliances without any hassles throughout your trip in Namibia.

Tipping and Bargaining

Tipping in Namibia:

Tipping is not necessary in Namibia, however it is appreciated for excellent service. If you are happy with the service given, you may provide a tip as a sign of thanks. Here are some tipping guidelines:

Restaurants: In restaurants, a tip of roughly 10% of the bill is usual if a service fee is not already included.

Safari Guides and Lodge personnel: Tipping safari guides, trackers, and lodge personnel is a regular practice. The amount is at your choice, but a recommended guideline is roughly 10-15 USD per day for guides and 5-10 USD per day for other staff members, depending on the quality of service.

Hotel Staff: If you experience excellent service at hotels or guesthouses, you may provide a little tip to the staff members who help you.

Porters and Drivers: For porters who carry your baggage and drivers who offer transportation services, a tip of a few dollars is appreciated.

Remember that tipping is totally discretionary, and you should never feel forced to tip if you were not happy with the service.

Bargaining in Namibia:

Bargaining is a prevalent activity at marketplaces and artisan stores in Namibia, particularly in more informal settings. Here are some strategies for bargaining:

Start with a Smile: Approach the discussion with a cheerful and courteous approach.

Know the Market Value: Before haggling, obtain a sense of the normal price range for the item you wish to buy.

Counter Offer: After the vendor offers you their original price, make a counteroffer that is lower but still fair.

Be Willing to Walk Away: If the seller's pricing does not fit your budget, be prepared to walk away.

Sometimes, the vendor may drop down on the price to make a transaction.

Be courteous: Bargaining is a cultural tradition, but remember to be courteous throughout the process and avoid getting overly forceful or confrontational.

Bargaining is more usual in rural markets and artisan stores, whereas set pricing is often provided in supermarkets, hotels, and more formal places.

Internet Access

Internet connection in Namibia has increased in recent years, notably in metropolitan areas and tourism attractions. Here's an overview of internet connectivity in Namibia:

Mobile Data: Mobile data is generally accessible across the country, and most regions have decent 3G and 4G coverage. Local mobile network providers provide data packages that travelers may buy for their cellphones or portable Wi-Fi devices.

Wi-Fi: Many hotels, lodges, guesthouses, and restaurants in major cities and tourism centers provide Wi-Fi connection for visitors. However, the internet speed and dependability might vary based on the area and the institution.

Internet Cafes: In major areas like Windhoek and Swakopmund, you may find internet cafes where you can use the internet for a price. These cafés are equipped with computers, and some also provide printing services.

Isolated places: In more isolated and rural places, internet connectivity may be restricted or unavailable. Whether you want to go to distant areas or national parks, it's advisable to verify in advance whether there will be internet connectivity at your hotel or nearby amenities.

SIM Cards: Tourists may acquire local SIM cards from mobile network providers like MTC or TN Mobile. This enables you to access mobile data on your smartphone, which may be helpful for remaining connected while on the road.

Public areas: Some public areas like shopping malls and tourist information centers may provide free Wi-Fi connection, however the quality and dependability might vary.

Internet Speed: While internet access has increased, the internet speed in Namibia may not be as quick as what you are accustomed to in more industrialized countries. Streaming and huge downloads may be sluggish, particularly in rural locations.

Keep in mind that although internet connectivity is accessible in many areas, it's always a good idea to have a backup plan for staying connected, particularly if you require dependable internet for business or other critical tasks. Consider checking with your hotel in advance to ensure their internet availability and speed if it's necessary for your vacation.

Cultural Etiquette

Cultural etiquette is vital while visiting Namibia, since it demonstrates respect for the local customs and traditions. Here are some ideas to assist you understand cultural standards and etiquette in Namibia:

Pleasantries: In Namibia, pleasantries are crucial, and a handshake is the most prevalent form of greeting in both professional and casual contexts. When welcoming someone, use the right hand, since the left hand is considered unclean.

Eye Contact: Making eye contact while speaking is a show of respect and attention in Namibian culture. It demonstrates that you are engaged in the discourse.

Dress Code: Namibians often dress modestly, particularly in rural and traditional regions.
When visiting villages or attending cultural activities, it is advisable to wear modest and polite apparel.

Respect for Elders: Respect for elders is highly prized in Namibian society. When addressing elderly folks, use their titles or suitable expressions of respect, such as "mama" or "tate" (father).

Public Displays of Affection: Public displays of affection, like embracing and kissing, are not frequent in Namibian society. It's preferable to keep demonstrations of love secret and modest.

Photography: Always ask for permission before taking images of persons, particularly in rural regions and among indigenous tribes. Some individuals may not feel comfortable with their photographs being taken.

Language: While English is commonly spoken, learning a few simple words in the local languages, such as hello and thank you, may be welcomed by the locals and enrich your cultural experience.

Traditional conventions: When visiting local communities or attending cultural events, be conscious of traditional conventions and practices. Follow the example of your hosts and seek help if you are confused about suitable conduct.

Gift Giving: If invited to someone's house, it is courteous to offer a modest gift, such as fruit, snacks, or a mark of gratitude.

Table Manners: When invited to a dinner, wait for the host to start eating before you begin. It is also polite to taste a little of everything presented, since it shows appreciation for the labor put into preparing the meal.

By obeying these cultural etiquette recommendations, you will show respect for the local culture and build great relationships with the people you encounter throughout your tour in Namibia. Remember that the Namibian people are typically friendly and inviting, and your attempts to be culturally sensitive will be well-received.

Fun Facts:

Namibia is a sanctuary for birdwatchers, with over 650 bird species, including the beautiful Lilac-breasted roller and the uncommon Rüppell's parrot.

EMERGENCY CONTACTS AND RESOURCES

Embassies and Consulates

In Namibia, multiple foreign embassies and consulates represent different countries. These diplomatic posts give aid and support to their residents visiting or living in Namibia. Here are some of the important embassies and consulates in the capital city, Windhoek:

United States Embassy:
Address: 14 Lossen Street, Ausspannplatz, Windhoek
Phone: +264 61 295 8500
Website: https://na.usembassy.gov/

British High Commission:
Address: 116 Robert Mugabe Avenue, Windhoek
Phone: +264 61 274 800
Website:
https://www.gov.uk/world/organisations/british-high-commission-windhoek

German Embassy:
Address: 29 Ruhr Street, Windhoek
Phone: +264 61 205 7111
Website: https://windhuk.diplo.de/

South African High Commission:
Address: 124 Robert Mugabe Avenue, Windhoek
Phone: +264 61 205 7111
Website: https://www.dirco.gov.za/windhoek/

Canadian High Commission (Accredited from Zimbabwe):
Address: 8th Floor, Old Mutual Centre, Windhoek
Phone: +263 4 758 800-810
Website:
https://www.canadainternational.gc.ca/zimbabwe/index.aspx?lang=eng

French Consulate (Honorary):
Address: 32 Fritsche Street, Windhoek
Phone: +264 81 124 4123
Website: https://na.ambafrance.org/

Please note that this is not a complete list, and additional countries may potentially maintain diplomatic missions in Namibia. For citizens of other countries, it is important to consult with their local embassies or consulates before traveling for the most up-to-date information and advice.

In case of situations affecting your country's people, these diplomatic offices may offer consular services, including aid with missing passports, legal concerns, and emergency repatriation. Always have the contact details of your embassy or consulate ready throughout your travels for any unexpected emergencies.

Medical Facilities and Emergency Services

Namibia has various medical facilities and emergency services accessible to cater to both inhabitants and tourists. Here's an overview of medical services and emergency aid throughout the country:

Medical Facilities

Hospitals: Namibia has governmental and private hospitals in major cities and settlements. Public hospitals provide healthcare services to Namibian people and are often more economical. Private hospitals offer more specialized and higher-quality treatment, generally sought by expats and tourists.

Clinics and Health Centers: Health clinics and centers are available in both urban and rural regions. They offer basic healthcare services, immunisations, and minor treatments.

Pharmacies: Pharmacies are widely available in towns and cities.

Many common prescriptions may be acquired without a prescription, but it's vital to visit a healthcare expert for more severe diseases.

Emergency Services

Ambulance Services: In case of medical emergency, contact 211 for an ambulance. Ambulance services are accessible in large cities and villages and may offer timely medical transportation to hospitals.

Emergency Contact Numbers:

Medical Emergencies: 211 (ambulance)
Police: 10111
Fire Department: 211
Medical Evacuation: For isolated places and significant medical situations, medical evacuation services may be necessary. Several commercial firms provide medical evacuation services in Namibia.

Health Precautions:

Immunisations: Before coming to Namibia, it's vital to consult with your healthcare practitioner for prescribed immunisations. Common immunisations include hepatitis A and B, typhoid, yellow fever (if entering from an infected region), and regular vaccines.

Malaria: Malaria is widespread in some places of Namibia, notably in the northern regions. It's vital to take malaria treatment and utilize insect repellent and nets while visiting these places.

Sun Protection: Namibia has a hot and sunny environment. Always use sunscreen, sunglasses, and a hat to protect yourself from the sun.

Drinking Water: Stick to bottled or filtered water and avoid drinking tap water to prevent waterborne infections.

Medical Insurance: It's important to have comprehensive travel medical insurance that covers medical emergencies, including evacuation if required.

In case of a medical emergency, seek urgent medical assistance or call the emergency services. Always bring critical medical information and your insurance data with you on your trip. It's also essential to research medical facilities and services in the locations you want to visit, particularly if going to more rural regions.

Fun Facts:

Adventure enthusiasts may enjoy exhilarating sports like quad riding in the desert, sandboarding down high dunes, and discovering ancient rock art sites.

CONCLUSION

In conclusion, my summer experience in Namibia was definitely amazing. Exploring the wide and different landscapes, from the towering dunes of Sossusvlei to the spectacular fauna in Etosha National Park, left me in awe of nature's magnificence. The guided trip enabled me to dive further into Namibia's rich history and culture, engaging with local people and observing their traditional way of life.

Throughout my travels, I accepted the local customs and cultural etiquette, demonstrating respect for the people and their traditions. I experienced the amazing native foods, learnt some words in the indigenous languages, and even tried my hand at traditional music and dancing.

The vacation wouldn't have been complete without the meeting with the fascinating black sky, stargazing in Namibia's black Sky Reserves, leaving me awestruck by the grandeur of the cosmos.

In addition to the amazing natural beauties, the journey was boosted by the kind friendliness of the Namibian people. Their warmth and willingness to share their tales made my trip all the more memorable.

As I think about my experiences, I am glad for the chance to have immersed myself in Namibia's beauty, history, and culture. The memories of this fantastic experience will long have a special place in my heart, and I want to return someday to see even more of this intriguing country. Namibia has left an unforgettable impact on my spirit, prompting me to appreciate the marvels of our planet and embrace the variety of its people.

Happy Travels!

Printed in Great Britain
by Amazon

38247731R00099